New Ways in Teaching Speaking

Kathleen M. Bailey and Lance Savage,
Editors

New Ways in TESOL Series
Innovative Classroom Techniques
Jack C. Richards, Series Editor
Teachers of English to Speakers of Other Languages, Inc.

Typeset in Garamond Book and Tiffany Demi
by Automated Graphic Systems, White Plains, Maryland
and printed by
Pantagraph Printing, Bloomington, Illinois USA

Teachers of English to Speakers of Other Languages, Inc.
1600 Cameron Street, Suite 300
Alexandria, Virginia 22314 USA
Tel 703-836-0774 • Fax 703-836-7864

Director of Communications and Marketing: Helen Kornblum
Senior Editor: Marilyn Kupetz
Editorial Assistant: Cheryl Donnelly
Cover Design: Ann Kammerer
Part Title Illustrations: David Connell

Every effort has been made to contact the copyright holders for permission to reprint borrowed material. We regret any oversights that may have occurred and will rectify them in future printings of this work.

ISBN 0-939791-54-4
Library of Congress Catalogue No. 94-060037

For Mark Dale, the world's most talkative kid,
who always makes me smile when he speaks.

Kathi Bailey

For my grandmother, Ameda Bryant, whose
love of good conversation has always warmed my heart.

Lance Savage

Contents

Acknowledgments

Many people have been helpful in generating this volume. First, of course, we wish to thank the contributors. Their enthusiasm for teaching is reflected in their writing. We are also grateful to John Esling, at the University of Victoria in British Columbia, Canada, who did the original editing of the pronunciation activities.

At the Monterey Institute of International Studies, where we work, we were greatly assisted with word processing by Jennifer Allen, Jennifer Goldsborough, Christy MacAnally, Aileen Gum, and Sheryl Black, who also helped manage the correspondence. Mary Davis and Julie Lonero dealt with huge photocopy orders and numerous international faxes.

In the TESOL Central Office, Helen Kornblum, Director of Communications and Marketing, and Marilyn Kupetz, Senior Editor, were informative and supportive. Finally, Jack Richards, Series Editor (and fastest fax in the East) believed in the project from the beginning.

Preface

Speaking in a second or foreign language has often been viewed as the most demanding of the four skills. When attempting to speak, learners must muster their thoughts and encode those ideas in the vocabulary and syntactic structures of the target language.

Depending on the formality and importance of the speech situation (and their own personal linguistic propensities), the learners may also attempt to monitor their output. In conversations and other interactive speech events, the speakers must attend to the feedback from their interlocutors and observe the rules of discourse used in the target culture. Phonological considerations add to the difficulty of the task, especially for adult learners, as speakers strive to achieve "good" pronunciation. The speed of such interaction is also an issue because there may not be adequate time for processing either outgoing speech or incoming messages at the typical rate of native-speaker interaction. All of these factors combine to make speaking in a second or foreign language a formidable task for language learners.

Yet for many people, speaking is seen as the central skill. The desire to communicate with others, often face-to-face and in real time, drives us to attempt to speak fluently and correctly. There is a dynamic tension caused by the competing needs for fluency and accuracy during natural speech. The varied difficulties learners face in speaking an L2 are addressed in the activities presented in this volume.

These activities in this book were developed by professional teachers who wished to help their students become better speakers of English. However, the procedures described here can be adapted to teaching any language. We hope that the diversity in the activities that follow will encourage language teachers around the world to try these and other new ways in teaching speaking.

Kathleen M. Bailey
Lance Savage
Monterey Institute of International Studies
Monterey, California
November 1993

Introduction

The intent of the New Ways series is to publish ideas written by teachers for teachers. This volume, *New Ways in Teaching Speaking*, focuses on several aspects of the macroskill of oral communication.

The book is organized into 4 parts, with 14 subsections. These divisions were not originally planned (although some were predictable). Instead, they emerged from the articles sent to us by teachers around the world. Some of the subsections are organized around pedagogic themes (Group Work, Dialogues and Role Play, Games for Speaking, and Using Audiovisual Aids). Others are organized around speech events or particular speech acts (Conversation, Oral Presentations, Spoken English for Academic Purposes, Functions in Speaking, Interviews and Questioning.) Other portions of the book are divided according to the subskills that influence spoken proficiency (Grammar, Vocabulary, Pronunciation, Fluency and Interaction). The sections of the books are meant to function independently, so that teachers may access activities for their own particular students' needs.

The view of speaking presented here is that of a demanding activity requiring the integration of many subsystems. The contributions to the book address various parts of these subsystems. The contributors were motivated largely by the desire to share ideas that had worked in their own classrooms with other professionals. The contributors' perspectives represent diverse points of view, both philosophically and practically, which we have not attempted to mold into any given framework or theory. Instead, we have organized the activities conceptually for ease of access.

Users' Guide to Activities

Group Work

Dialogues and Role Plays

Games for Speaking

Using Audiovisual Aids

Part II: Accuracy

Functions

Grammar

Vocabulary

Part III: Pronunciation

Segmental Phonemes

Suprasegmental Phonemes

Part IV: Speaking in Specific Contexts

Oral Presentations

Spoken English for Academic Purposes

Interviews and Questioning

Part I: Fluency

◆ Conversation
Talking Zone

Levels
Any

Aims
Practice low pressure
conversation
Develop fluency,
friendship, memory,
cooperation

Class Time
Variable

Preparation Time
Variable

Resources
Handouts from the
teacher or students'
own papers
Pens or pencils

This activity blends ideas related to information gap and read-and-look-up activities as well as to personal space and physical movement. It allows students to converse with a large number of classmates and to have time to remember; rehearse privately, reflect on, and make decisions about what they will say and hear. It requires students to share, collect, and understand information by speaking and listening and then record the information in writing. The students can discuss just about anything you think they are capable of discussing without having it in writing at the moment they are speaking.

Procedure

1. Divide the class into two "zones."
2. Have the students converse in one area (talking zone) and read and write in the other (recording zone).
   - Students may stay in either area as long as they wish and may return to either area as often as they wish. They may speak with whomever they want for as long they want provided they are in the talking zone and are speaking to only one person at a time in the target language.
   - They may look at their own papers in the recording zone whenever and for as long as they wish, but they may not look at their classmates' papers or speak there, and they may not take their papers, pens, or pencils into the talking zone.
3. If your classroom has movable furniture, empty one area (to be filled shortly with standing, speaking students). One possibility is to have the middle encircled by chairs, with the recording zone against the four walls.

4. If your classroom has immovable furniture, designate the front, back, sides, or isles as the talking zone.
5. Then, with your students in the recording area (sitting or standing), hand out or dictate the questions or topics that they will discuss.
6. Tell them to write their own short responses to each item before going into the talking zone to begin speaking.

Caveats and Options

1. One idea for the handout is to have a chart with columns for the student's own response, two students who responded the same way, and two students who responded differently. In the latter two columns, the students' names will need to be recorded, and in the last column, their responses as well. Also, you can embed additional questions/topics in these latter two columns where appropriate. You can have more than one set of questions/topics at the same time if you would like. Another idea is to use newspaper articles or short reading passages, maybe three to five at one time. After talking with a partner who read a different article, students return to their papers and are given some questions to answer about their partner's article. Any unknown information needs to be collected through further discussion back in the talking zone.
2. If students forget information, questions, or topics, they need to go back to the appropriate area to get it.
3. The first time you use this, you may need to enforce the rules (e.g., where to do what and to speak only in English).
4. Later on, occasional reminders may also be necessary, but try to keep out of the way as much as possible. You can sit and observe, videotape, or wander around inconspicuously collecting errors or accurate language samples.
5. If you only want half of your students talking at once, tell them to pair up; one of the pair will collect the information in the talking zone while the other waits in the recording zone. Then the talkers must return to the recorders to tell them what to write. They can switch roles half way through.
6. By announcing a time limit before the students begin, the activity can be made into a competition.

7. Some students may reduce their conversational contributions to single words. If you really think they can do better, give them a gentle reminder that the main purpose of the activity is to practice conversing not to just collect the required information. However, remember that some students need more time to begin speaking freely than others.

References and Further Reading

Bresnihan, B. (1992). How is at least as important as what. *The Language Teacher, 16,* 37–41.

Gorsuch, G. (1991, January 31). Working around students' cultural traits. *Daily Yomiuri*, p. 9.

Contributor

Brian Bresnihan is currently an instructor at Kobe Shouka Daigaku in Japan. He has also taught in New York City, Tokyo, and Hiroshima.

Don't Drop the Ball

Levels
Any

Aims
Learn the unspoken
rules of conversational
interaction in an
enjoyable, memorable
way
Use gambits to
stimulate conversation
and repairs

Class Time
5–10 minutes

Preparation Time
None

Resources
Lightweight ball
(e.g., a tennis ball)

In this activity, the familiar child's game of catch is used as a metaphor for conversational activity to illustrate the implicit rules of this type of interaction. The playfulness of the activity creates a memorable impression in the learner's mind of the expectations of listeners and speakers and allows the learner to recognize potentially inappropriate behaviors. The activity is also a good technique for teaching interviewing skills and to illustrate the disasters that await those who ask only yes-no questions. As students catch on, they'll often take over the lead in this game, tossing the ball to classmates and loudly chastising them for failure to follow the "rules."

Procedure

1. Use this as a class opener. When all the students are seated, greet someone warmly and ask a routine question, such as, "Did you have a good weekend?"
2. As you finish the question, gently toss the ball to the student who, you hope, will catch it.
3. If the student doesn't answer the question, silently retrieve the ball and repeat the question and ball toss.
4. When the student answers the question, signal that you want the ball tossed back.
5. If the student only answers the question with "Yes" or some similar short response, then don't catch the ball—let it drop to the floor and stare at it morosely as it bounces away.
6. After a brief dramatic pause, sigh and retrieve the ball.
7. Ask the same student a new question: "Where did you go?" and toss the ball again.

8. Continue doing this until the student finally includes some countering gambit in response: "To the movies. How about you?"
9. When the student asks you a direct question, beam happily and catch the ball.
10. Now direct a question or comment to another student, and continue until everyone has caught on to the "rules" of conversation.

Caveats and Options

1. Devise different responses to illustrate various aspects of the conversation system:
   - Take the ball indignantly from someone who talks too long.
   - Stop tossing the ball back to someone who never indicates reciprocal interest in you as a conversational partner.
   - Make a great show of retrieving the ball and restarting the game when you must use some kind of "repair" to keep a conversation going.
2. When training students to interview a resource person, use the ball activity to demonstrate the consequences of asking yes-no versus information-seeking questions. Let the ball game demonstrate how the interviewer controls the flow of talk in an interview.
3. This can quickly become a rowdy activity, so keep it short—use it to make your point, but then put the ball away.
4. You can repeat it later—or simply refer to it in passing—any time students seem to be forgetting the rules of conversation.

Contributor

Alice Gertzman teaches ESOL and trains teachers at Georgia State University in the United States.

Circle Conversation

Levels
Any

Aims
Develop fluency by
balancing the risk of
free conversation with
the security of a
structure

Class Time
10–15 minutes

Preparation Time
None

Resources
None

Many students, especially low-level learners, either will not volunteer to speak or will have difficulty choosing a subject. The Circle Conversation activity provides students with a subject and promotes a semifree conversation.

Procedure

1. Ask students to sit in a circle. For a large class, first demonstrate Circle Conversation with a small circle (12–20 students), and then have the other students make additional circles.
2. Nominate a topic and say something about it. For example if the topic is coffee, you could say, "I usually drink about three cups of coffee a day" or more simply "I like coffee."
3. Have the student sitting to the left of the teacher continue by saying something about the same subject. (It is permissible but not necessary to include the topic word.)
4. Do not permit students to ask questions at this time. In this way the speaker's turn moves around the circle with each student talking about the same subject. Unless the teacher imposes a time limit, students may say as little or as much as they please.
5. When everyone has spoken, have the student to the left of the teacher nominate a new subject and say something about it. In this way, not only does the speaker rotate but so does the role of topic initiator.

Caveats and Options

1. Prepare a pack of subject cards. On each card write a one-word topic or a short phrase.
2. When the turn comes to Student A, he or she draws a card and makes a statement, thereby nominating a subject. (The student can also ask

for the next card.) For low-level classes in Japan, these card topics have worked well:

A good pack of Circle Conversation topic cards would have 50–60 cards.

3. For high-level classes, cards might include the same topics listed above but also items such as the following:

4. Keep blank cards in your pack for inclusion of new topics; throw away any topics that don't work.
5. Provide students phrases to indicate they are finished speaking (such as "That's it.") so the next student knows when to begin.
6. In Circle Conversation, the main job of the teacher is to keep things moving. Decide whether it is necessary to limit long-winded speakers.

Contributor

Dale T. Griffee teaches at Seigakuin University, Japan. His latest books are Songs In Action *(Prentice Hall, 1992) and* More Hearsay *(Addison-Wesley, 1992).*

Talking to Yourself

Levels
High beginning +

Aims
Show understanding of
the interlocutor's
meaning and feeling
Increase sensitivity to
appropriate timing for
giving feedback and
backchanneling

Class Time
20–30 minutes

Preparation Time
20–30 minutes initially

Resources
Recording equipment
Backchanneling handout

Even advanced learners (particularly in EFL situations) may feel uncomfortable and unnatural in conversation with native speakers, especially when more than one native speaker is taking part in the conversation. The skills of giving feedback and backchanneling to show understanding of both meaning and feeling are vital to making conversation enjoyable.

Procedure

1. Create a handout with formulaic feedback and backchanneling comments such as the following:
   ● Uh-huh
   ● Uh-uh
   ● Huh?
   ● Oh*
   ● Sorry?
   ● Pardon?
   ● Really*
   ● I see. (I'm with you so far)
   ● Now I get it.
   ● You're kidding!
   ● Isn't it? (Doesn't she? etc.)
   ● You must be tired. (happy, etc.)
   ● How disappointing! (exciting, etc.)
   *For these gambits, be sure to show students the different meanings involved with different intonation.
2. Give each student a copy of the handout.
3. Model the meaning and pronunciation (especially suprasegmentals) of each formula. It may be worthwhile to make some sample conversations in which the examples are used.

11

4. Have each student talk for 5–8 minutes, without stopping their recorders. Any topic is fine, and changing topics is fine. The main thing is that the students talk and record continuously for 5–8 minutes.
5. At the end of recording time, have the students rewind their tapes and listen to themselves, giving feedback wherever they can.
6. Have the students pay attention to pauses in their recorded speech because pauses are often natural places for giving feedback or backchanneling.
7. Monitor the students and make suggestions where appropriate, especially if students are letting too many opportunities for feedback pass by.
8. Have students repeat Step 5, to see if they can improve their first effort.

Caveats and Options

1. Introduce only a few formulas at a time, to keep from overloading the students. (Add to the students' repertoires of comments each time the exercise is done in class.)
2. Help the students understand that the sincerity of the person giving feedback or backchanneling is often judged on pronunciation (especially suprasegmentals) and that a change in stress and intonation can indicate completely different intentions.
3. Another format for this activity is good for pair work.
   - Pair off the students and designate a main speaker and a listener.
   - Have the class brainstorm topics and write them on the board.
   - Have the pairs talk for 5 minutes (the main speaker should carry the conversation, while the listener keeps track of the number of times he or she gives feedback or backchannels).
   - After 5 minutes of conversation, ask the students for their running record of feedback to monitor increased usage.
   - Have students switch roles and repeat the last two steps above.

Contributor

Kenny Harsch is Director of English Education at Kobe YMCA College, in Japan. He is interested in students developing uses for English, learner autonomy, and student-centered curriculum development.

First Steps and Sidestepping

Levels
Intermediate +

Aims
Practice introducing
and changing subjects
naturally

Class Time
10–15 minutes

Preparation Time
None

Resources
None

Many learners say that it is very difficult to feel comfortable or natural about conversation in an L2. Changing the subject is often handled with abruptness by learners or with overuse of a formula (such as *by the way*). This activity allows students to practice one of the main ways native speakers change the subject: They say something that relates their tangential subject to the current subject (i.e., using something about the current subject to sidestep to their own subjects).

Procedure

1. Brainstorm topics of interest for students. (Make sure students understand that the topics should be ones they feel comfortable talking about for at least 5 minutes.)
2. Write the students' topics on the board.
3. Divide the class into pairs with no pair of students sharing the same topic.
4. Explain the rules of the game as follows:
   - Have each student talk about a topic for part of the 10-minute talking time.
   - Have students start and change topics in an indirect manner only (i.e., no one can start or change the topic with e.g., *I'd like to talk about . . .* or *Let's talk about . . .* or *By the way . . .*).
   - Students can change back and forth between their two topics as many times as they'd like during the 10 minutes of talking time, but only in an indirect manner relating to the tangential topic.
   - Students receive one point for introducing their topics to start conversations, and one point for each time they sidestep the conversation to their topics (when done smoothly), and one point if their topic is discussed for most of the 10 minutes.

5. Have students begin talking while you listen in and help where needed.
6. Stop the students at the end of 10 minutes, having them count up their points and declare a winner in each pair.

Caveats and Options

1. It may be useful the first time students play this game if you introduce some natural, indirect ways of starting and changing topics. You can say something about the topic itself or demonstrate sidestepping to a new topic by relating it to the original topic.
2. Instead of putting students into pairs, put them into threesomes and have the third student serve as monitor and score keeper while the other two students talk.
3. After the game is over, remind the students that conversation is usually more fun for both people when it is cooperative, not competitive.

Contributor

Kenny Harsch is Director of English Education at Kobe YMCA College, in Japan. He is interested in students developing uses for English, learner autonomy, and student-centered curriculum development.

Taking Control of a Conversation

Levels
Intermediate +

Aims
Practice subtly
redirecting a
conversation to a new
topic
Increase sociolinguistic
awareness

Class Time
30 minutes

Preparation Time
10 minutes

Resources
Sentence strips
Pencil and paper

An important conversational skill is being able to quietly take control of the conversation to bring it around to a topic of one's choice. Because language learners sometimes seem to introduce totally unrelated topics, this activity provides students with practice in the art of subtle command of a conversation.

Procedure

1. Explain the rationale of the activity to students by demonstrating that some kinds of phrases effectively cut the speaker off and can be offending (e.g., overly abrupt uses of *by the way*).
2. Demonstrate how to change subtly from one topic to another by making an association or link between a current topic and the next topic in a conversation. Model making these associations by saying a word and choosing a student to say a word that has a connection with your word (e.g., *elephant* and *grey*).
3. Have each student take a turn making an association with the word given by the previous person.
4. To make connections at the sentence level, have each student write two unrelated sentences on a piece of paper.
5. Pair off students and have Student A read the first sentence to Student B, who must form an association with his own first sentence so that he can introduce the sentence naturally into the conversation. (e.g., the first student's sentence might be *I like Mac computers,* and the second student's sentence could be *I have a Mac but couldn't use it yesterday because I went to a movie.*)
6. Have students change roles using their second sentences.

15

7. In preparation for the next part of the activity, create sentence strips (one for each student). The more abstract the sentences, the more fun and challenging the activity.
8. Give each student a strip, pair off the class, and instruct partners not to show one another the sentences.
9. Have students talk about some teacher-determined topic only (e.g., the ozone layer), for about 1 minute.
10. After 1 minute, have the students begin to maneuver the conversation toward a topic that will facilitate the natural introduction of the sentence on their strip into the conversation. (To do this, students have to form links between the initial topic and each other's sentences.)
11. The first students to say their sentences verbatim in a natural manner are the most skillful at redirecting the conversation.
12. Have the students who get to their sentence first explain to the class the strategies they used to accomplish the task.

Caveats and Options

1. You can have some students work as topic shift monitors while the others converse in pairs. The monitors' job is to listen to their classmates' strategies for changing topics and then to report back to the class.
2. After doing this activity, have students listen to conversations and note examples of topic shifts, and then report to the class.
3. Students can also listen for topic shift strategies in television programs.

Contributor

Lesley Koustaff has been working in Japan for 9 years. She is a language school director and candidate for an MA in ESL.

Express Yourself With Balloons

Levels
Intermediate +

Aims
Practice conversational
fluency and emphasize
emotion
Interact in informal
social situations

Class Time
1½ hours

Preparation Time
None

Resources
One large balloon/
student
Magic markers

The range of natural emotions that could occur in a conversation of native speakers of English is often reduced to a monotonous exchange by nonnative speakers who are afraid to make fools of themselves by appearing too emotional. This is especially true of any theatrical activity in which the student has to act out a script in front of the class. But if the students blow up a balloon, draw a person, animal, or object on it and then hold that balloon in front of their faces, they will begin to identify with and be what they created. In doing so, the majority will tend to lose their fear of looking foolish and begin to experiment with the full range of emotions displayed by native speakers.

Procedure

1. Divide the class into small groups (maximum four students per group). One good way to form groups is to have students pick numbers out of a hat and have all four students that pick the same number work together.
2. Have each group think of a topic and characters for their balloons (e.g., people, animals, or cartoon characters).
3. Have students write and practice a conversation to take place between their characters with a time limit of 5–10 minutes for each group's conversation.
4. Help each individual group if grammar or vocabulary problems arise.
5. Have each group practice their conversation and perform the short scene/conversation for the class while holding their balloons in front of their faces.

Caveats and Options

1. This game can be tailored to fit your students' creativity level and can be adapted to intermediate English fluency levels and above by structuring the exercise (e.g., offer prepared topics or characters consistent with the group's ability or based, perhaps, on a language skill that has been covered in class debating, or expressing emotions such as sympathy or joy).

2. What students draw on the balloons is of course not as important as what they say and how they say it, so take some time to make the following comments:
   - Assure students that their balloons do not have to be works of art.
   - Encourage students to concentrate on the emotions and thoughts they want to express in their conversations. In this way, you can give the students individual attention and discuss with them the various possibilities an English native speaker has, both in word choice and in intonation, for expressing a single idea.

References and Further Reading

Behma, H. (1985). *Miteinander Reden Lernen-Sprechspiele im Unterricht*. Munich, Germany: Iudicium Verlag GmbH.

Contributor

Rachel Baron Lester has taught EFL in Germany at high school, at college, and in adult education. She currently teaches EFL and American Culture at the University of Munich.

Planned Conversations

Levels
Low intermediate +

Aims
Develop fluency in
extended conversation
within a familiar,
practiced context

Class Time
15 minutes/group

Preparation Time
30–40 minutes

Resources
Paper

When engaging in casual, seemingly free conversation in our L1s, we usually have a shared base of knowledge and awareness of the participants' background. It can be difficult to get students to transfer these often unconscious skills to another language, particularly in a large class. This activity sets up parameters and allows opportunities to simulate authentic conversation.

Procedure

1. Divide the class into groups of four to seven students, and have each group list half a dozen topics about which they normally converse and would like opportunities to discuss in English (e.g., summer vacation, getting a driver's license, high school days, love, urban life, AIDS).
2. Give the following parameters for conducting the conversations, and model them with examples:
   - a plausible opening
   - turn taking
   - at least one change of topic
   - a plausible closing
3. Tell students that their conversations will be judged on fluency, preparation, equal participation, and natural flow of topics.
4. Have each group prepare to have a conversation in front of the class on any of the topics on their list. Because students do not know which topic they will present as a conversation, preparation should not entail memorization of lines but a general outline for each topic. Encourage students who have trouble speaking to get coaching from their group members. (Set aside time to practice all the topics on a group's list either in class or as homework.)

19

5. Choose one topic from one group's list and have those students conduct a conversation in front of the class for 10–15 minutes.
6. You and the other students in the class should provide feedback on vocabulary gaps and grammar points that interfere with the meaning the group members try to get across.
7. Repeat the procedure with each group so that all have a chance to present and give feedback.

Caveats and Options

1. This activity works well if it is used in conjunction with the teaching and practice of various aspects of discourse (e.g., openings, closings, clarification, gambits, and turn taking).
2. Set up an alternate scenario for conversation based on practicing and explaining various cultural aspects to someone from outside a culture. This activity is helpful for students who anticipate traveling abroad and having a need to explain unique aspects of their native culture.
   - Have each group make a list of three to five topics from their own culture that they wish to be able to explain, in English, to someone from outside their culture (e.g., fireworks, school regulations, *omiai* [Japanese arranged marriage], *otoshidama* [money received by Japanese children at New Years]).
   - Using the conversational parameters from the exercise above, have the groups develop notes for conversation using English language travel guidebooks, newspaper and magazine articles on the native cultural topics of choice.
   - Assume the role of cultural outsider, and have each group explain one of the topics to you in 10–15 minutes.

Contributor

Margaret Pine Otake is Director of a private language school in Japan and also teaches at two Japanese universities.

Students as Language Researchers

Levels
Intermediate +

Aims
Understand conventions
of conversational turn-
taking system in U.S.
English
Notice differences and
similarities between
English and students'
L1s

Class Time
1–3 hours

Preparation Time
1–2 hours

Resources
Audiotape recorder
60–minute audiotapes

Audio- and videotapes make available to us the means to "freeze" natural language interactions. This can be useful in heightening learners' awareness of their own language behavior and of what actually happens in normal, everyday conversation. Such an activity encourages more realistic attitudes toward error and accuracy because native speakers' informal speech is normally filled with inaccuracies. The activity also offers ways to learn about and practice conversation strategies that contribute to smooth and coherent conversation flow.

Procedure

1. Prepare a sample transcript (2–3 minutes worth) from a taped conversation and demonstrate the process to students.
2. Have students choose a native English speaker with whom they are familiar and record a 30-minute spontaneous conversation with that person.
3. Have students listen to the taped conversation and choose two short (2–3 minute) excerpts to transcribe: one that they consider a "smooth" interaction and one where they encountered some kind of problem (e.g., a point where the native speaker did most of the talking and the learner had trouble getting a turn, or a breakdown of communication where the learner did not understand a term used by the native speaker).
4. Have students work with their transcripts and tapes in small groups, each with a tape recorder.
5. Have students describe the problems they encountered and play the tape so the group can discuss what could have been done to alleviate the problem interactions (e.g., What could the learner have said to

21

break into the conversation or to indicate lack of comprehension?), and also discuss the contrasting aspects of the successful interactions.

6. Discuss and model with the whole class the conversation strategies that nonnative speakers typically have trouble with (e.g., active back-channeling to indicate interest in what the speaker is saying; turn-claiming devices; expressing the need for clarification or restatement).

Caveats and Options

1. Conduct a follow-up role-play activity for small groups, with one person acting as the observer who makes notes on aspects of the interaction while the other two students take on the roles of conversation participants.
   - Have the observer focus on specific conversation strategies (e.g., backchanneling), and note how the participants respond, verbally and nonverbally.
   - Have the observer give feedback to the speakers and report observations in a large group discussion.
2. If you have access to audiotapes of native speaker-nonnative speaker conversations, prepare beforehand samples of common nonnative speaker problems in conversations as examples for students.
3. In countries where there is little access to native English speakers, students can hold conversations with fluent or advanced learners instead.
4. In active high-level conversation classes, this activity can carry itself. More structured follow-up activities may be required for intermediate or less active classes.

Contributor

Heidi Riggenbach is Assistant Professor in the University of Washington's MA TESL program. She has taught ESL teachers and students in the United States, China, and Malaysia.

Word Routes

Levels
High intermediate +

Aims
Express opinions about
a subject and refer to
events freely
Ask questions and seek
opinions

Class Time
15–20 minutes

Preparation Time
30 minutes

Resources
List of interesting topics

This activity can make students feel more relaxed about expressing their opinions among their own peer groups. It generates a lot of talking as students are free to express whatever ideas/opinions they have about a topic. It allows freedom and flexibility so students develop confidence in their speaking and fluency skills as they examine the twists and turns that different conversations can take on the same subject.

Procedure

1. Prepare a list of topics that interest students (e.g., fashion, taxes, toothpaste).
2. Divide the class into several groups of five or six students.
3. Have students choose one member of the group to take notes.
4. Give all the groups the same topic for free discussion. (This means students are free to discuss the topic and to develop and carry on their conversation within the time limits of the activity.)
5. While students are discussing the topic, have the note-taker keep track of the progression or "word route" of the conversation (e.g., from toothpaste, to teeth, to dentists, diet, to clothes).
6. At the end of the time period (5–10 minutes), check the groups' progress and have the note-taker of each group present the word route they have recorded.
7. Compare the different groups' development of their conversations as a whole-class activity.

Contributor

Matilda M. W. Wong is Assistant Lecturer in the Department of English, City Polytechnic of Hong Kong. She holds an MA in ELT from the University of Warwick, England.

Three-Minute Conversations: Getting to Know You

Levels
Any

Aims
Get to know classmates
Practice conversation
skills

Class Time
1 hour

Preparation Time
15 minutes

Resources
Movable desks
Timer with bell
Handouts with world
map, topics of
conversation, and
recording list (see
Appendices below)

This is a great activity for the first week of class when the students are short of books and confidence. The skills practiced are initiating, continuing, and closing a conversation; asking and answering questions; and communicating information. Students have an opportunity to get to know each other in a nonthreatening environment—all of which is necessary if the students are to feel free to speak up later in the semester.

Procedure

1. Arrange half the desks in a large outer circle facing in and the other half in an inner circle facing out so that when seated, every student will be facing a partner.
2. Give the students 3 minutes to discuss the topics listed on the handout in the style of a normal conversation, as if each one started with a friendly stranger at a bus stop.
3. Model a conversation with a student and point out that the conversation goes back and forth from person to person; one student does not simply read all his answers to another student.
4. At the end of 3 minutes, when the timer sounds, ask the students on the inner circle to stand up and move one seat to the right to begin another 3-minute conversation with a new partner.

Caveats and Options

1. One hour is needed for a class of 30. The introduction to the activity and the arranging of the seats take about 15 minutes. If there are 30 students, it takes 45 minutes for the activity itself because there are 15 pairs speaking for 3 minutes each.

2. Participating in nonstop conversations is exhausting, so limit the activity to 1 hour, the time it takes for a class of 30 to make a full round to meet 15 other students.
3. Ask that both students take turns to practice keeping the conversation going. Students may ask any other questions that come up; the object is not to race through the questions and finish but to get to know each other.
4. If there is an odd number of students, you may participate or ask the student who sits at the desk without a partner to be the time keeper. This allows for each student to get a 3-minute break and get a chance to observe the incredible verbal and nonverbal interaction taking place all over the room.

Appendix A: World Map Handout

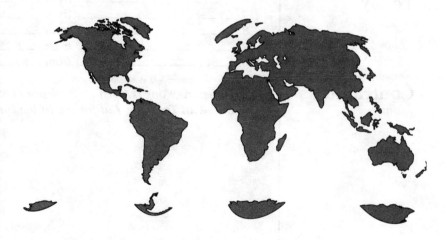

Appendix B: Topics of Conversation Handout

1. Greeting (e.g., *Hi, how are you?*)
2. Name (If it is a difficult name you might ask: *How do you spell that?*)
3. Country (Make sure they know where it is on the map)
4. Length of time in the United States (e.g., *How long have you been here?*)
5. Family situation (e.g., *Do you live with your family? Are you married? Do you have any children?*)

6. Occupation/Major (e.g., *Are you working? What's your major in school?*)
7. Any interesting question (e.g., *If you could be anywhere in the world right now doing anything you wanted, where would you be and what should you be doing?*)
8. Closing (e.g., *It was nice talking to you. Let's talk again later.*)

Appendix C: Sample Handout: People I Met Today

1. _____ from _____
2. _____ from _____
3. _____ from _____
4. _____ from _____
5. _____ from _____
6. _____ from _____
7. _____ from _____
8. _____ from _____
9. _____ from _____
10. _____ from _____

Contributor

Mary Shepard Wong is Assistant Professor of ESL at El Camino Community College, in Torrance, California, in the United States.

Two-Minute Conversations:
If I Were . . .

Levels
Any

Aims
Get to know classmates
Practice the conditional

Class Time
45 minutes

Preparation Time
15 minutes

Resources
Movable desks
Timer with bell
Handout with 15 or
more categories (see
Appendix below)

This activity gives the students the opportunity to get to know each other better and therefore helps to create a nonthreatening environment for speaking and sharing ideas. It also encourages students to think creatively because they must share a personal characteristic in an abstract way. Students practice initiating, continuing, and closing a conversation; using the conditional; communicating personal information; and developing vocabulary.

Procedure

1. Arrange half the desks in a large outer circle facing in, and the other half in an inner circle facing out so that when seated, every student has a partner.
2. Give the students 2 minutes to discuss the topics listed on the handout. There is a different topic for each conversation but every conversation starts with the phrase, "If I were a _____ , I would be (a) _____ because _____ ." (e.g., If the topic were Body of Water, they could say, "If I were a body of water, I would be an ocean because an ocean can be very calm, deep, and mysterious, but in a moment's notice it can be raging and dangerous. That's the way I am, very moody, but never dull. How about you? What would you be?" or if the topic were Color, the student might say, "If I were a color, I would be green because I feel like I'm growing and changing a lot this semester.")
3. At the end of 2 minutes, when the timer sounds, ask the students in the inner circle to stand up and move one seat to the right to begin another 2-minute conversation with a new partner.

Caveats and Options

1. The introduction to the activity and arranging the seats takes about 15 minutes. If there are 30 students, it takes 30 minutes for the activity itself because there are 15 pairs speaking for 2 minutes each.
2. Have the students write about their favorite category by writing a paper that begins "If I were a . . . ."
3. If there is an odd number of students, you may participate or ask the student who sits at the desk without a partner to be the time keeper. This allows each student to get a 2-minute break and get a chance to observe the incredible verbal and nonverbal interaction taking place all over the room.
4. If it is a beginning class, preteach the vocabulary and allow the students to use the examples on the handout.
5. You might want to preteach the use of the present unreal conditional and the use of articles with count versus noncount nouns (e.g., "I would be *a hamburger*, and I would be *fruit*.")
6. If it is a more advanced class, the students are required to come up with their own examples, not those on the handout, which adds an extra element of challenge.

Appendix: Handout for 2-minute Conversations: If I Were . . .

If I were (a/an) _____ I would be (a/an) _____ because _____

1.	Shape:	triangle	square	hexagon	oval
2.	Food:	vegetable	fruit	rice	meat
3.	Drink:	water	maitai	beer	coke
4.	Color:	jet black	lavender	turquoise	shocking pink
5.	Car:	sports car	sedan	truck	limousine
6.	Animal:	tiger	fox	rabbit	monkey
7.	Clothing:	scarf	sock	belt	nightgown
8.	Doctor:	pediatrician	dentist	internist	plastic surgeon
9.	Book:	Bible	mystery	diary	best seller
10.	Building:	gas station	store	school	house
11.	Flavor:	strawberry	chocolate	mocha	cinnamon
12.	Vehicle:	boat	motorcycle	bike	bullet train
13.	Body of water:	river	lake	stream	ocean
14.	Dwarf in *Snow White*:	Sleepy	Bashful	Grumpy	Dopey
15.	lower:	daisy	daffodil	rose	lily
16.	Pizza:	pepperoni	plain	the works	extra cheese
17.	Body part:	nose	ear	eye	hand

18.	Object:	scissors	chair	pillow	window
19.	Appliance:	dishwasher	refrigerator	dryer	microwave
20.	Music:	classical	pop rock	soft rock	jazz

Contributor

Mary Shepard Wong is Assistant Professor of ESL at El Camino Community College, in Torrance, California in the United States. This activity is an adaptation of Gertrude Moskowitz's (1978) "Suppose You Weren't You" in Caring and Sharing in the Foreign Language Class *(Newbury House).*

◆ Fluency and Interaction
Creative Common Ground

Levels
Beginning–intermediate

Aims
Speak spontaneously
through experimental
poetry and drawing
Practice interaction and
verbal exchange

Class Time
30 minutes

Preparation Time
5–10 minutes

Resources
Chalkboard or chart
paper
Chalk, colored pencils,
or markers
Blank paper

The challenge of teaching beginning-level students largely lies in finding common ground among the students' diverse cultural backgrounds. Creative word play can offer that common ground because of its visible imagery.

Procedure

1. Present an example of a simple word written creatively. (e.g., *man* may be shown with the actual letters of the word forming an image. See below.)

2. Have students decipher the shape in a guessing game.
3. Have the students play with the letters of their names, arranging and manipulating them in an interesting and unique design as in the figure below. (Students can draw them with colored pencils or use cut out letters.)

4. Have students show what they have created to the rest of the class.
5. Provide other nouns, verbs, and prepositions to extend the exercise.
6. Next, have the students select words from books and magazines, or choose words they already know (e.g., the preposition *over*, where the letters *ver* are curved above the letter *o*, suggesting the meaning of the word as in the figure below.)

7. Have the students justify their designs and interpret each other's work. (This creates an ideal setting for spontaneous verbal communication and interaction, and is a valuable tool for expanding vocabulary.)

Caveats and Options

1. Put students into groups of various sizes and creative media (e.g., paper cutting, drawing) and have the groups interpret and evaluate each other's work.
2. You can also have the students form complete sentences. Check the sentence shapes for structure and correct word order.

Contributor

Catherine Adkins teaches multilevel ESL classes in Toronto, Canada. She previously taught in Egypt for 5 years.

Nonstop Dream House

Levels
Any

Class Time
20–30 minutes

Preparation Time
None

Resources
None

Gatbonton and Segalowitz (1988) explain how repetition in communicative activities can lead to automatization, one component of fluency.

Procedure

1. Have students draw floor plans of their dream houses in class or as homework. They should include furnishings and make their plans as detailed as possible.
2. Pair off students.
3. Have one student in each pair explain his dream house floor plan while the other student listens. The goal is to talk for 1 minute without stopping or switching into the L1.
4. After 1 minute, have the students switch parts with the first student in each pair listening and the second student talking nonstop for 1 minute.
5. The first student in each pair should move one seat over to form a new group.
6. Repeat Steps 3–5 until all students have talked to each other or time runs out.

Caveats and Options

1. Choose other topics for students to talk about. They can bring in family pictures or childhood pictures. They can talk about hobbies or topics selected at random by the teacher or student.
2. You may want to demonstrate the activity by describing your dream house to the students at the beginning of the activity.
3. As students repeat the same information over and over, they will build up confidence. They will repeat the same utterances several times, be able to say more and more in the same amount of time, and increase their fluency.

32

References and Further Reading

Brumfit, C. (1984). *Communicative methodology in language teaching*. London: Cambridge University Press.

Gatbonton, E., & Segalowitz, N. (1988). Creative automatization: Principals for promoting fluency within a communicative framework. *TESOL Quarterly, 22*, 437–492.

Rooks, G. (1983). *Can't stop talking*. Rowley, MA: Newbury House.

Contributor

Linda Deines works at Concordia College, in Tokyo, Japan.

Demystifying the TSE/SPEAK Exam

Levels
Intermediate +

Aims
Make short, impromptu
responses to practice
for the TSE/SPEAK
exams

Class Time
2 minutes/student/
activity

Preparation Time
1 hour

Resources
Flash cards
Picture stories, comic
strips, pictures of
scenes with people, and
announcements of
scheduled events
Overhead projector
(OHP)
Transparencies
Stop watch

Although we can argue about the merits of the TSE and SPEAK exams, many students preparing to enter the university and the business community are required to take them. Using this activity, instructors can relieve some of the anxiety created by these tests through short warm-up activities that benefit even those students not facing the exams. The procedures below follow the format of the TSE/SPEAK exams in that students are given 1 minute (or less) to respond to these types of cues.

Procedure

1. Create flash cards (see Appendix below).
2. Pass around the deck of flash cards face down and have students take turns taking the top card and completing the activity on the card. (You may want to model one card of each activity type for the class before beginning.)
3. After the flash card activity, put a picture, comic strip, picture of a scene, or schedule of events on the OHP for individual students to discuss. Some examples include:
   - Picture Narration (2 minutes): Have students study a sequence of pictures on the overhead for 1 minute. In round robin style or individually, have students narrate the story for 1 minute.
   - Picture With Questions (2+ minutes): Have students study one picture of a scene involving people for 1 minute. Ask questions about the picture to elicit different verb tenses (e.g., *Where is this scene taking place?* or *What has just happened?*), and have the students respond in complete sentences.

● Schedule (2 minutes): Have students study a schedule for an event for 1 minute. Call on one or two students to give an informal presentation of the information as if they were speaking to a group.

Caveats and Options

1. You may or may not want to go over some errors or problems after the activity (e.g., not using time well).
2. Students who are under pressure to take these exams can be given cards/pictures to practice in a language lab setting for later evaluation.

Appendix: Creating Flash Cards

1. Create three different sets of cards:
   ● Sentence completion cards contain half of a sentence (usually a dependent clause) and students must read and complete the sentence correctly within 15 seconds.
   ● Description cards contain the name of an object (e.g., bus, refrigerator, library) or a concept (e.g., a perfect day, an interesting custom), and students must talk about it for 1 minute as a response.
   ● Opinion cards contain a problem (e.g., world hunger, pollution) that students must "solve" in 1 minute.
2. The flash cards can be combined into one deck for distribution to students in the activity.

Contributor

Susan Earle-Carlin teaches in the ESL and TESL Certification Programs at the Irvine campus of the University of California in the United States.

Three Steps to Comprehension Checks

Levels
Low intermediate +

Aims
Use comprehension
checks effectively
Identify confusing
information in an
utterance
Make appropriate
conversational repair

Class Time
30–40 minutes

Preparation Time
Task 1: 10–15 minutes
Task 2: 1 hour
Task 3: 30 minutes

Resources
Imagination
Materials for worksheets
(See Appendices)

Negotiation of meaning is essential for L2 acquisition. In order to negotiate meaning, learners need to be able to make conversational repairs using comprehension checks, confirmation checks, and clarification requests. In the typical ESOL curricula and course books, expressions for realizing these functions are often presented at the beginning of the course as classroom English along with many other words and expressions. Learners may then be given some tasks that provide opportunities to practice the expressions. Unfortunately, a step tends to be missing: intermediate tasks that develop a student's ability to identify the problematic features of an incomprehensible utterance.

The three tasks presented here are sequenced so that the chore of making comprehension checks is broken down into its component parts.

Procedure

Task 1: Identifying Questionable Information in Sentences
1. Create a worksheet with 7–10 items, each containing three sentences, some of which have inaccurate information.
2. Two of the sentences in each item should contain incorrect or odd information (e.g., Pigs can fly), but the information in the third sentence should be accurate (e.g., Birds can fly).
3. Either you or a student should read one of the three sentences aloud.
4. Have students mark the sentence they heard on the worksheet and underline any part of a sentence they feel is inaccurate or questionable.
5. Help the students to come up with useful comprehension check items about the questionable information (e.g., *Did you say pigs can fly?*).

36

Task 2: Identifying Questionable Information and Selecting Comprehension Checks

1. Give students a worksheet of comprehension checks on a 10 x 10 grid (see Appendix A).
2. The information on the grid is correct, but give incorrect oral directions to the students (see Appendix B) for each successive number on the grid in order to elicit one of the confirmation checks listed for that number on their worksheet.
3. The students check the teacher's oral directions against the numbers written on the grid and then select the appropriate comprehension checks for that item. For example: Number 1 is actually in the C-4 square, but you say, "Put Number 1 in the C-5 square." Looking at the multiple choice items below the grid, the students should then mark (a) on their worksheet, representing the comprehension check "Did you say C-5?" As students correctly query the erroneous oral instructions, confirm their understanding.

Task 3: Making Comprehension Checks

1. Pair off the students, with one student in each pair having an "A" identity and one having a "B" identity.
2. Distribute a worksheet (A or B with grid and directions, see Appendix C) to each pair of students, giving Student A in each pair the worksheet marked A and giving Student B in each pair the worksheet marked B.
4. Have the students read the set of directions on their worksheets to each other, taking turns.
5. Students should make the necessary corrections to the directions they are using to match the numbered grid of their partner's worksheet: Student A reads the directions about Student B's grid and Student B listens and compares the directions to Grid B; Student B should use comprehension checks to confirm what she hears and instruct the partner to change the erroneous information in the written directions to the correct form.

Caveats and Options

1. The number of items for a task can be altered to meet various situational needs (e.g., students can fill the roles of the teacher in task one and two if time is not a factor).
2. This sequence of tasks has been used with first-year high school students with a great deal of success. The problem-solving nature of the tasks matches the problem-solving nature of learning and using an L2, which makes the components of the comprehension check more salient.
3. These tasks assume that the learners are familiar with the directives necessary for doing the grid work (e.g., "Go up two squares and left three squares").

Appendix A

Did you say go up two squares?

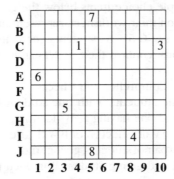

1 2 3 4 5 6 7 8 9 10

1. a. Did you say the C-5 square?
   b. Did you say go up?
   c. Did you say go down?
   d. Did you say go right?

2. a. Did you say go up two squares?
   b. Did you say go down two squares?
   c. Did you say go left two squares?
   d. Did you say go right two squares?

3. a. Did you say go down four squares?
   b. Did you say go right four squares?
   c. Did you say go up four squares?
   d. Did you say put the number 4?

4. a. Did you say put the number 5?
   b. Did you say go up five squares?
   c. Did you say go down five squares?
   d. Did you say go left five squares?

5. a. Did you say go up five squares?
   b. Did you say put the number 5?
   c. Did you say go down five squares?
   d. Did you say go right five squares?

6. a. Did you say go down two squares?
   b. Did you say go up two squares?
   c. Did you say go right two squares?
   d. Did you say go left two squares?

7. a. Did you say go left four squares?
   b. Did you say go up four squares?
   c. Did you say go right three squares?
   d. Did you say go down three squares?

8. a. Did you say go right seven squares?
   b. Did you say go down seven squares?
   c. Did you say go up seven squares?
   d. Did you say put the number 7?

Appendix B

Sentences (misdirections read for the task)	Correct responses
1. Put the number 1 in the C-5 square	a.
2. Go down three squares and left two squares. Put the number 2.	c.
3. Go up four squares and right four squares. Put the number 3.	c.
4. Go left two squares and down six squares. Put the number 5.	a.
5. Go right five squares and up two squares. Put the number 5.	d.
6. Go down two squares and left two squares. Put the number 6.	a.
7. Go up four squares and right three squares. Put the number 7	c.
8. Go down seven squares. Put the number 8.	b.

Appendix C

Student A

Step 1: Read the directions to your partner and correct the mistakes your partner finds in the directions.

First, put the number 1 in the B-3 square.
Next, go left two squares and down two squares. Put the number 2.
Now, go up five squares and left two squares. Put the number 3
Now, go left eight squares and down four squares. Put the number 4.
Next, go down six squares and put the number 5.
Now, go right four squares an up two squares. Put the number 6.
Then, go up six squares and left four squares and put a 7.
Now, go down three squares and right four squares. Put the number 9.

Step 2: Listen to your partner compare the directions with the numbers on the grid. **The numbers on the grid are correct**. If the directions are wrong, tell your partner to change the directions.

Step 2 grid

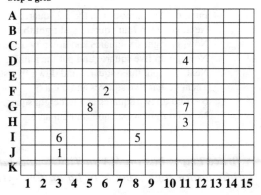

Student B

Step 1: Listen to your partner compare the directions with the numbers on the grid. **The numbers on the grid are correct**. If the directions are wrong, tell your partner to change the directions.

Step 1 grid

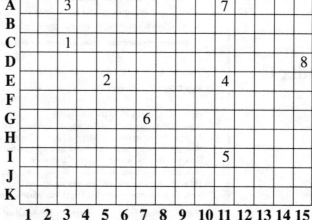

Step 2: Read the directions to your partner and correct the mistakes your partner finds in the directions.

First, put the number 1 in the J-2 square.
Next, go down four squares and right three squares. Put a 2.
Now, go right six squares and down two squares, and put a 3.
Now, go up five squares and put the number 4.
Next, go right three squares and down five squares. Put a 5.
Then, go left five squares and put a 6.
Next go up two squares and left eight squares. Put a 7.
Now, go right six squares and put an 8.

Contributor

Bruce Evans has an MA in TESOL and has been teaching English in public junior high schools in Japan for 7 years.

Negotiating Meaning Through Dictation

Levels
Any

Aims
Practice negotiating
meaning

Class Time
45–60 minutes

Preparation Time
30 minutes

Resources
Several short texts at
suitable reading level
Handout with strategies
for negotiating meaning
(see Appendix below)

People are constantly negotiating meaning in discourse, to clear up what Ur (1984) terms *gaps* in listening. In their L1s, people learn to negotiate meaning naturally, but these skills don't automatically transfer to an L2; learners need practice. This exercise is designed to make students aware of the negotiation process, expose them to some ways of negotiating meaning in English, and give them practice with these skills.

Procedure

1. Explain negotiation of meaning. Make sure the students understand that these are strategies for making listening easier. (If you like, have two students who speak the same L1 talk naturally in their L1 to highlight the two-way nature of their conversation.)
2. Explain the first strategy on the handout, Interrupt, and give examples.
3. Hand out texts and put students into pairs.
4. Have half the students dictate their texts to their partners. Have the listening partner write down what is being dictated using the strategy to negotiate meaning wherever necessary. (Make sure the one who is writing cannot see the original text.)
5. After the students have finished the dictation and writing, have them check the copied version against the original for errors.
6. Follow the steps above for each remaining strategy on the handout.
7. After all the strategies have been explained and students have practiced them, give each student a new text. Explain that this time the students can use all of the negotiation strategies to help them produce an error-free copy.
8. Put the students into pairs again and follow the same procedure for dictation as above. This time, after they've finished, students either

41

grade their own work or hand in their dictated copies and originals for you to grade.

Caveats and Options

1. Give each pair of students a full text, half to one partner and half to the other. After they've done their dictations, have each partner read the text individually and decide which half comes first. Further activities based on the text can follow.
2. Have each pair of students record the interaction. You can listen to the tapes for grading the ability of students to negotiate meaning, rather than relying on what is overheard and the number of errors on the copy.
3. These activities are easier to use for ESL than EFL because students who don't have the same L1 will probably be forced to negotiate meaning in English to perform the task. If you are using it for EFL students, it may be easier to record the interactions to ensure that students aren't using their L1.

References and Further Reading

Ur, P. (1984). *Teaching listening comprehension*. Cambridge: Cambridge University Press.

Appendix: Strategies for Negotiating Meaning

1. Interrupt
   To stop the speaker, use
   - Excuse me or Pardon me
   - Sorry
   - Um or Could I interrupt?
2. Question Whether You Heard Correctly
   Repeat the words or sentence you are unsure about using a rising intonation at the end.
3. Ask the Speaker to Repeat
   Repeat the part you heard and ask a question about the part you are unsure about, such as
   - You went where? or She's a what?
4. Give Feedback to Show You Understand

When the speaker pauses slightly, use these expressions to show that you understand

- Uh-huh or M-m h-mm

5. Control the Pace of Conversation

Speak slowly yourself to show the speaker the pace you are comfortable with or ask the other person to speak more slowly.

6. Ask for Full Repetition

Asking someone to repeat a whole paragraph can be very frustrating in a conversation. For small pieces of language only, use

- What was that? or Could you repeat that?

Contributor

Kenny Harsch is Director of English Education at Kobe YMCA College in Japan. He is interested in students developing uses for English, learner autonomy, and student-centered curriculum development.

Round Table Discussion

Levels
Intermediate +

Aims
Generate
comprehensible input
for each other
Build fluency by
recycling a topic
Integrate reading,
writing, and speaking
skills

Class Time
2 hours

Preparation Time
None

Resources
None

Caveats and Options

This activity allows students to develop topics and ideas for group discussions and to clarify and play with the language items they have created. If students generate the input themselves, there is a good chance it will be comprehensible. Additionally, the desire to understand and be understood can be enhanced if students discuss topics important to them. More negotiation of meaning can take place in this manner and can help students make both input and output comprehensible (see, e.g., Pica, 1987; Pica, Holliday, Lewis, & Morgenthaler, 1989).

Procedure

1. Have students write a paragraph about something they think is important. (Brainstorm examples with the class or make some suggestions of your own.)
2. Put students into small groups and have one student read his or her paragraph to the group. (Group members can ask for clarification at any time.)
3. Have the groups discuss the topic for 5–10 minutes after each reading.
4. Once all the students have had an opportunity to read and have their topic discussed, rotate people into different groups and do Steps 2 and 3 over again.

1. The rotations can take place over several class periods and be adapted to any content or theme as a unit activity.
2. As an alternative procedure, do the following:
   - Collect the written paragraphs and put them in a box.
   - Have one member of each group draw a sample from the box for reading and discussion as above.

- Have each student in the group write their thoughts about the topic and give them to the person who originated the topic.

References and Further Reading

Pica, T. (1987). Second language acquisition, social interaction, and the classroom. *Applied Linguistics, 8*, 1–25.

Pica, T., Holliday, L., Lewis, N., & Morgenthaler, L. (1989). Comprehensible output as an outcome of linguistic demands on the learner. *Studies in Second Language Acquisition, 11*, 63–90.

Contributor

Kenny Harsch is Director of English Education at Kobe YMCA College in Japan. He is interested in students developing uses for English, learner autonomy, and student-centered curriculum development.

Presidential Conversations

Levels
Intermediate +

Aims
Practice paraphrasing
and restating written
information orally

Class Time
30–45 minutes

Preparation Time
5 minutes

Resources
Deck of biographical
picture cards (see
References and Further
Reading below)

In Presidential Conversations, students develop fluency in English through an information-gap activity using a set of biographical picture cards about the presidents of the United States. The activity also increases reading comprehension, vocabulary, and knowledge of the history and the political system of the United States. This activity effectively elicits English from students because students enjoy handling these cards, looking at the pictures, and talking to new discussion partners.

Procedure

1. Select a chronologically ordered series of cards from the *Presidents of the United States* card deck (two cards per student are best). The cards have biographical information printed on one side and a portrait of a president on the other.
2. Shuffle the cards and distribute two to each student.
3. Explain that students must find the classmates who are holding the cards that describe the presidents preceding theirs (e.g., a student who happens to draw the cards describing the thirty-third and twenty-third presidents must find the students with the cards about the thirty-second and twenty-second presidents).
4. Have the students read their own cards silently.
5. Tell the students to move around the room, comparing cards.
6. Have students orally exchange one fact about each president (after finding the classmate with the card about the president preceding theirs) by paraphrasing the information on their card.
7. Lead a class discussion by asking students to volunteer new information they have learned during this activity.

46

Caveats and Options

1. Have students exchange information about themselves in addition to facts about the presidents.
2. Beginning students may read from the card rather than paraphrasing the information.
3. Because the cards are marked with each president's political party, this activity can lead to a class discussion of the party system in the United States.
4. Student conversations can supply material for vocabulary lessons.

References and Further Reading

The biographical picture cards *Presidents of the United States, Kings and Queens of Great Britain,* and *The Old West From A-Z* (illustrated with art work about the American West), are available from FAX-PAX USA, Inc. at 203-242-3333. The cards can also be found in museum shops and bookstores.

Contributor

Michele Kilgore is an ESL instructor at Georgia State University in the United States. She has an MS in Applied Linguistics and is working on her doctorate.

Real Problems

Levels
Intermediate +

Aims
Practice interacting
Solve problems in
English

Class Time
30–60 minutes

Preparation Time
None

Resources
None

This activity motivates students to develop communicative competence because it is based on student-identified needs. The focus on sharing problems and creating solutions together fosters an atmosphere of trust and cooperation in the classroom. The students' reservoir of practical knowledge about living in the United States increases. This activity is particularly effective in a university setting because students can easily get to different parts of the campus to collect information, and fill out applications.

Procedure

1. Have students select a partner. (Partners should not have the same L1.)
2. As a warm-up exercise, ask students to discuss the minor, daily problems caused by living and going to school in a foreign country.
3. Ask students to choose one personal problem with a definite solution (e.g., the student may need information about taking a driving test, choosing a dentist, studying for the GRE, using public transportation, or learning to use a computer).
4. Have partners discuss ways to solve each other's problems and create a plan of action.
5. Act as an information resource to check the feasibility of the plans.
6. Ask for volunteers to share their problems and solutions with the class.

Caveats and Options

1. Have pairs of students use the time before the next class period to implement their plans. They can report their solutions to the group.
2. Lead a class discussion about the results of the problem-solving exercise.

3. Have students write a paragraph explaining how they helped their partners.
4. Have students give short oral reports on the progress of their problem-solving activities later in the course.

Contributor

Michele Kilgore is an ESL instructor at Georgia State University in the United States. She has an MS in Applied Linguistics and is working on her doctorate.

Eavesdropping Journal

Levels
Intermediate +

Aims
Develop perceptive
listening skills and
incorporate what is
heard into speech

Class Time
5–10 minutes

Preparation Time
5 minutes

Resources
Native speakers
Lined paper

There are many ways that students can work on their language skills outside of the classroom, but sometimes these opportunities need to be pointed out. This activity guides students in the discovery of one possible way.

Procedure

1. Explain and discuss eavesdropping and how students can learn from paying attention to the speech of others.
2. Give an eavesdropping assignment for homework where students listen in on one or several conversations.
3. Have students jot down information such as:
   - where and when the conversation occurred
   - who the speakers were
   - what they were talking about
   - any new vocabulary
4. Give students a sample format for recording the information:

   Where: Dunkin Donuts
   When: Saturday afternoon
   Speakers: Customer and counter person
   Topic: Donuts. Customer asked for a baker's dozen.
   New terms: *Baker's dozen* (13), *glazed donuts*

5. During the next class, have students form small groups and use their notes to retell the conversations they have overheard. Have students explain the new vocabulary and report their observations.

Caveats and Options

1. Students should be advised not to eavesdrop obtrusively.
2. Give a more specific focus by asking students to eavesdrop on speakers of a certain age group or sex and have students compare and contrast the topics of conversation and the kind of language used.
3. Have students observe and contrast social interaction between adults, teenagers, parents and children, and so forth.
4. An eavesdropping session could also include focusing on reduced speech or nonverbal communication.

Contributors

Sally La Luzerne-Oi has taught in Mexico, Venezuela, Portugal, and Japan. She is currently an instructor at Hawaii Pacific University in the United States. Jean Kirschenmann has taught in Micronesia, Romania, and China and is now an instructor at Hawaii Pacific University.

Multilevel Interaction

Levels
Any

Aims
Improve spoken
language skills of
students at different
levels by interacting
with each other and the
instructor

Class Time
10–20 minutes

Preparation Time
5 minutes

Resources
Advertisement that
portrays people as well
as the product being
sold

The multilevel classroom presents a unique challenge to an ESOL teacher used to a group of students working through a syllabus or a book at the same pace. Students learn at different rates and employ various strategies. Students may also acquire different skills, resulting in a group that has some members who may be proficient in reading, while others may read poorly but be able to speak quite well.

This activity addresses the needs of mixed proficiency classes with advertisements. In these exercises, the focus is on the message rather than on a specific set of grammar points. The students at various levels can understand the material on a range from what sort of material it is (lower levels) to specific details (intermediate to higher levels).

Procedure

1. Reproduce copies of the advertisement for the students or allow the whole class to see it as a poster.
2. Have the students give a basic description of the product. For example, they can discuss its color, number of people in the advertisement, and so forth.
3. If the target structure is *be* for instance, and the advertisement is for a car, ask questions about the people in the advertisement, the shape, color, model, age of the car: *Is it a truck or a car? Is it expensive?*
4. With more advanced learners, do Steps 1 and 2 above and then add structures to describe what the people are doing, will do, or have done. (e.g., *Will you buy the product? How much would you pay? Do you like it?*).
5. At even higher levels, do Steps 1–3 and then discuss the roles the product plays in the culture.

6. After the oral work, have students write their own impressions or read an article related to the product. For example, they may find something about cars and transportation, home electronics, computers, or other information that interests them.

Caveats and Options

1. If you are working with international students studying ESOL in the United Kingdom, the United States, Canada or Australia, have them contrast the role of the object in the picture in their home culture and in their host country.
2. Do not let the structure (grammar) part of the discussion become mere repetition or drill. Make sure the students at the different levels understand that there is a right way to say things, but don't dwell too long on discrete points.

References and Further Reading

Bragger, J. D., & Rice, D. B. (1984). *Allons-y! Le français par étapes.* Boston: Heinle & Heinle.

Dunkel, P. (1986). Developing listening fluency in L2: Theoretical principles and pedagogical considerations. *Modern Language Journal, 70,* 99–106.

Krashen, S. D., & Terrell, T. D. (1983). *The natural approach.* Oxford: Pergamon.

Contributor

Douglas R. Magrath teaches ESL at Seminole Community College and provides ESL workshops for teachers in Volusia County, Florida in the United States. He has published in Foreign Language Annals, Selected Articles from the TESOL Newsletter, *and* Teaching English to Deaf and Second Language Students.

The Fluency Workshop

Levels
Intermediate +

Aims
Speak fluently and
naturally

Class Time
30 minutes

Preparation Time
10 minutes

Resources
Watch or timer
Chalkboard and chalk

Most speakers tend to pause a lot and use many fillers when they speak, especially when talking about a topic for the first time. As we speak more about a topic, these pauses and utterances tend to decrease. This activity has three elements: (a) discussing the same topic three times; (b) discussing it with three different partners; and (c) and discussing it in shrinking time frames. By talking about one topic in class three times, students can improve their fluency skills. Changing partners enables each speaker to talk in a meaningful way to someone new. The shrinking time frames allow students more time in the beginning of the activity to think about the topic, while pushing students to speak more fluently and naturally toward the end of the activity.

Procedure

1. Choose a few topics for class discussion that are interesting to and at the level of your students.
2. Pair off the students and assign half the students Topic A and the other half Topic B.
3. Explain the rationale of the activity and draw a chart like the one below on the board.

	A person/topic	B person/topic	Changeover
Partner 1	4 minutes	4 minutes	1 minute
Partner 2	3 minutes	3 minutes	1 minute
Partner 3	2 minutes	2 minutes	Finish

4. Have A students speak about their topic for 4 minutes to one B student. (Speakers commonly struggle in the first 4 minutes, but encourage them to keep speaking and encourage the listeners to ask questions to keep the speakers talking.)
5. Be the time keeper and stop the discussions at the appropriate time.
6. Staying with the same partner, have B students speak about their topic for 4 minutes to the A students.
7. During a 1-minute changeover, rotate students to form different A/B pairs, and repeat the discussion process for 3 minutes.
8. Rotate students to form different A/B pairs and repeat the discussion process for 2 minutes.
9. Monitor the time and listen for recurring errors and interesting content that can be used for later discussion. Clarify important points at the changeovers, if necessary.

Caveats and Options

1. Use this activity for many kinds of topics, grammatical points, communicative functions, and purposes (e.g., preparing students to give public speeches or to debate).
2. Include listening tasks as well (e.g., note-taking, summarizing and reporting).
3. For lower level classes, reduce the speaking times so that students can gain confidence.
4. For large classes, put students into small groups not pairs.
5. It is important to tell students the rationale, and it is advisable to link this activity to the specific functions or larger tasks of reinforcement or preparation for something more difficult (e.g., public-speaking).

References and Further Reading

Maurice, K. (1983, August). The fluency workshop. *TESOL Newsletter*, p. 29.

Contributor

Keith Maurice is Assistant Director at the Center for Intensive English Studies at Florida State University in the United States. He has taught in Japan and Thailand.

Daily Activities in Speaking

Levels
Intermediate

Aims
Practice describing
daily activities
Utilize high frequency
words fluently

Class Time
5–10 minutes

Preparation Time
None

Resources
Notebooks
Pencils

In this activity, students give a detailed description of a process selected from common daily activities. The purpose of the detailed account is to encourage the students to use thematically related vocabulary and consider the stages involved in carrying out the process described. The activity also brings everyday life into the classroom, thereby making the lesson more entertaining. The timely provision of a list of appropriate words and phrases motivates the students to enlarge their present vocabulary.

Procedure

1. Choose a topic that is performed in stages and that is familiar to the students. For example, making tea is a familiar activity performed through certain stages (First you boil water, then ...). You may select a topic or have the students give their ideas. Several topics can be selected in advance and written on slips of paper that students then draw from a hat, bowl, or bag.
2. For this particular topic, give the following sample sentences:
   * I spent a difficult day at work.
   * I was very tired and thirsty.
   * I wanted to make tea for myself.
   * I pushed open the door of the kitchen ....
3. Have the student(s) tell the procedure in chronological order, either in pairs, in small groups, or in front of the class. Draw the students' attention to the necessity of detail in the stories.
4. Add a list of possible words or phrases concerning the topic. (These can be written on the chalkboard as you elicit the steps from the students, or you can prepare the list in advance, either on the chalkboard, on a printed handout or on an overhead projector transpar-

ency.) For example, the following infinitive phrases might all be used in describing the process of making tea:

- to open the cupboard
- to take the kettle
- to take the lid off
- to turn the water on
- to turn the water off
- to put the lid back on the kettle
- to turn the gas on
- to put the kettle on the gas stove
- to turn the gas off
- to strike a match
- to light the gas
- to boil the water
- to pour the tea into the cup

Give the students the list of words that should be included in the stories after they finish. The students can easily see the useful words and phrases that may have been missing from their own accounts. This list is useful for enriching vocabulary (particularly common words) and practicing grammar items (e.g., conjunctions).

Caveats and Options

1. Other familiar activities include making a long distance telephone call, riding a bicycle, taking a bus, and mailing a letter.
2. If a student describes the activity but leaves a stage unsaid when working with a partner, have the second student supply the missing stage. (This creates cooperation among the students.)
3. If the students are speaking before the class, after each story have the students in the audience ask follow-up questions. In the example given above, for instance, someone might ask the students why it was a difficult day.
4. Have students write the steps of a familiar procedure on strips of paper or index cards. These can then be shuffled or scrambled and other individuals or pairs of students can sort them into their proper sequence.
5. Have individual students describe procedures that are familiar to them but may not be well known by their classmates. Such procedures

could include sports activities (e.g., waxing a pair of skis, hitting a golf ball), cooking, performing a craft (e.g., folding origami paper, weaving, knitting), building or making something. In classes with students from diverse cultures, this task can be quite informative.

6. Narratives can be used as well as procedures for practicing chronological order and cause and effect. For example, students can continue a story that begins as follows: "It was cold and rainy. The street was as silent as death. Then a young girl appeared. She was carrying a suitcase . . . . "

Contributor

Oya Tunaboylu teaches speaking skills to freshman at the Faculty of Education, Ataturk University in Erzurum, Turkey. Her interests include developing new techniques for English speaking classes and motivating students.

◆ Group Work
Where's the Beef?

Levels
Any

Aims
Warm up before
shopping activities
found in commercial
textbooks

Class Time
1½ hours

Preparation Time
None

Resources
Chalkboard and chalk
Blank paper and pencils

One of the most popular activities in language teaching today is the communicative task in which students plan an event or a visit. An event might be a camping trip or party; a visit might be to a town or country. Likewise, a very popular unit in commercial textbooks today is that of a shopping lesson. This activity combines these two ideas and can serve as a useful warm-up lesson for a shopping unit. In this activity, the students design a floor plan of supermarket displays.

Procedure

1. Explain that students may need to go food shopping while visiting a foreign country, and it may be beneficial to learn about the supermarkets and the products sold there.
2. Write on the chalkboard some of the products that are normally found in a supermarket, and then elicit and write down the students' suggestions.
3. Have the students categorize them (e.g., dairy products, meats, fruits, vegetables).
4. Place the students into groups of three or four.
5. Draw the outline of a store on the chalkboard, with an entrance marked in the lower left corner and an exit marked in the lower right corner.
6. Off to the side of the skeleton floor plan, draw four or five small squares to represent cash registers, and several rectangles representing freezers, refrigerators, and shelves that can be placed in the store later by the students. (There should be nothing in the interior of the store.)
7. Have the students draw the same outline on their papers.

8. Have each group draw the freezers, refrigerators, and shelves in the most suitable places inside the store. Students can then place various products and foods in the appropriate locations on the shelves and freezers.
9. Have the groups consider how to best satisfy customers' needs while stocking their supermarket. (Remind the students that they can use the front of the shelves and cash register areas for display purposes.)
10. Introduce some useful expressions for the groups to use as they negotiate their floor plans. Some examples include:
    ● I think the bread should go here because it is close to the peanut butter.
    ● The toys should be placed next to the cash register because . . . .
11. After the groups have designed the supermarkets, change the groups and have each student discuss their original group's design with the new partners.

Caveats and Options

1. Have each group bring their design to the front of the class for a presentation.
2. For a follow-up activity, find some pictures of supermarkets from the United States or another country and compare them with the students' layouts.
3. For a reading option, find information that describes how supermarket managers display their wares, and the logic behind their displays.
4. The vocabulary categorizing activity may be done in groups instead of being directed by the teacher.

Contributor

Robert M. Homan is an instructor at International Christian University in Tokyo, Japan. His interests include cooperative language learning and the teaching of speaking skills.

Creating a New Country

Levels
Intermediate +

Aims
Develop small-group
interaction skills

Class Time
Variable over several
sessions

Preparation Time
15–20 minutes

Resources
Basic art supplies (e.g.,
poster paper, scissors)

Collaborative, content-oriented, and task-based approaches to L2 learning have been shown to be very productive. This activity combines the advantages of all three in a motivating, noncompetitive task, focused on geography and social science. It includes procedures to ensure equal participation of each group member.

Procedure

1. Outline the borders of an imaginary country and make enough photocopies for the class.
2. Explain the nature of the project and put students into small groups.
3. Distribute a copy of the outline of the imaginary country to each group.
4. Explain that groups are free to design the geography, detail the climate, describe the nature of the people, the government, the economy, and the social practices (e.g., schooling, religion).
5. Have the groups choose different members to be responsible for particular aspects of their assigned country.
6. During each class session devoted to this project, the individual in charge of the given topic is responsible for directing the group's discussion and should come prepared with questions to guide fellow members and to keep the group on task. (Emphasize that individual preparation for these days is essential for facilitating group discussion.)
7. Afterwards, the individual who led the discussion of the day should review his or her notes and write up a coherent description of the topic to pass out to each group member at the next meeting.
8. Each aspect of the country is covered in turn by different members of the group.

9. The final class session is devoted to each group naming their country, creating a national flag and a large scale map (using basic art supplies).
10. When the groups are ready, have each group introduce their country in a 20-minute panel format similar to the following:
    - Each member takes 2–3 minutes to deliver part of the presentation.
    - Save several minutes at the end for questions from the audience.
    - Students should think of themselves as official representatives of their countries and should dress accordingly. (This, along with the formality of the presentation, lends a more realistic feeling to the activity.)
11. The students are graded on their weekly participation in groups (as observed by the teacher) as well as their final presentation, including the quality of their map and national flag.

Caveats and Options

1. Designate a "Prime Minister" for each group to be in charge of seeing that the group is staying on task (especially when less proficient or quiet individuals are in charge of the discussion). This person can also submit a grade for each individual for total group participation.
2. Videotape the presentations and watch them in class as a way for students to evaluate themselves.
3. For attention to form and pronunciation, have the panel presenters write and practice their short lecture beforehand (e.g., with a teacher or a lab tutor).

Contributor

Mark James has taught ESL for 12 years and is currently Director of the TESOL Studies Program at Brigham Young University-Hawaii, in the United States.

The Environmentally Sound Town

Levels
Any

Aims
Discuss a politically
sensitive topic
Reinforce
contextualized
vocabulary use

Class Time
30–50 minutes

Preparation Time
15 minutes

Resources
Black line map of a
fictitious town
Tape and scissors

The objective of this activity is for the students to work together and decide how to build an environmentally sound town. This activity should follow others that teach about the environment. It incorporates a variety of vocabulary items, the functions of persuading, giving and defending opinions, and compromising, as well as oral presentation skills.

Procedure

1. Distribute one map for every three students.
2. Give a list of things that they will need to include in their town. This list should include innocuous things like a shopping center, school, nursing home, and apartment houses, as well as less desirable things like a nuclear power plant, a paper factory, a highway, and a garbage dump.
3. Give students three blank spaces in the options for planning a town. Students fill in the blanks and choose what they want the characteristics of their town to be.
4. Have students work together in groups of three or four and then present their plan for a town to the class. Have them explain why they made the decisions they did.

Caveats and Options

1. Students can read about a town with environmental problems and brainstorm possible solutions to those problems.
2. Invite a guest speaker from a utility company or an environmental organization to visit your class. Help the students prepare to ask questions of the speaker by anticipating the contents of the presentation.

3. Have students discuss three environmental benefits and three ecological problems in the area where they live.
4. Discuss the pros and cons of apparent polluters (e.g., of the nuclear power plant in the area).

Contributor

Elizabeth Macdonald was a Peace Corps Volunteer in the Central African Republic and has trained EFL teachers for the Peace Corps. She received her MA in TESOL at the Monterey Institute of International Studies, where she is Director of the Intensive ESL Program.

My Partner Said

Levels
Intermediate +

Aims
Reduce anxiety about
speaking in front of
class

Class Time
30 minutes

Preparation Time
None

Resources

Reading texts
Pictures, cartoons

Some students feel too intimidated to present their ideas orally in class. This activity creates a comfortable setting for students so they can feel more at ease when they are reporting another person's ideas. In this activity, students are encouraged to develop effective oral presentation skills.

Procedure

1. Pair off students, have them pick a text, picture, or cartoon and discuss the material together. (Texts and materials can include short stories, poems, articles, excerpts from a book, paintings, caricatures.)
2. Have students decide what their own interpretation of the material is and then exchange these ideas with their partners.
3. Have each student retell the partner's comments back to the partner, who is in an "active listening" mode. The partner can interrupt at any point during the narration to negotiate misinterpretations of his original point of view.
4. Divide students into small groups and ask one student in each group to summarize all the other points of view.

Caveats and Options

1. To emphasize reading comprehension, divide students into pairs and give them a 5-minute in-class assignment to read a text. (The text can be a poem, short story, article, excerpt from a book or newspaper.)
2. Ask Student A in each pair to interview Student B for 5–10 minutes about the text, focusing on Student B's point of view. Encourage Student A to ask questions about Student B's views and negotiate terms with Student B. Student A can take short notes but should not write down everything Student B says.
3. Have Student A in one of the pairs report on Student B's view to the class, emphasizing accuracy, conciseness, and clarity.

4. After Student A has finished reporting, have Student B comment on and rectify any misinterpretations in Student A's presentation.
5. Repeat the activity with the other pairs of students in the class.
6. When all the pairs have reported, lead the class in a discussion of the reasons and possible remedies for any inaccuracy that occurred in the oral retransmittal of ideas by a second person.
7. Ask one student in each pair to summarize a film seen by their partner or discuss a popular topic instead of giving them a text.

Contributors

Selda Mansour teaches freshman English courses, and Wisam Mansour is Assistant Professor in the English Language and Literature Department at Eastern Mediterranean University in Cyprus.

Storytelling With Pictures

Levels
Any

Aims
Create and tell stories
cooperatively

Class Time
20–40 minutes

Preparation Time
Variable

Resources
Picture file

This activity is an expansion of the Show and Tell game.

Procedure

1. Put students into groups of four people.
2. Have each student pick one picture from the file.
3. Have each group choose a scribe to keep notes.
4. Have the group create a short story using all four pictures, and have the scribe take written notes about the group's story. (Model this procedure with some unused pictures.)
5. Have the group choose one or more members to tell their story to the whole class, holding up the pictures for illustration.

Caveats and Options

1. Add an extra picture to a group's collection to further complicate the story.
2. If a group can't agree on one story, have them produce separate stories and share both with the class.

Contributor

Myrtis Mixon, storyteller and video lover, has taught and told stories from New York to California, as well as in Russia and Indonesia. She is now teaching at City College and the University of San Francisco in the United States.

◆ Dialogues and Role Plays Conversation Creation

Levels
Beginning–intermediate

Aims
Learn new vocabulary
Practice style and
register differences
Plan discourse

Class Time
5–10 minutes

Preparation Time
Variable

Resources
Chalkboard and chalk
or overhead projector
(OHP), pen, and blank
transparency

This activity draws on cognitive skills to produce appropriate language in context. It originated in an effort to have students (with the same L1) speak only in English for 2 class hours a day. The opening dialogue can serve as a daily ice breaker, one that students have come to expect and look to in order to guess the day's topic or structures.

Procedure

1. Write a two-person conversation on the board (or OHP). If new vocabulary is being introduced in the lesson, include it in the conversation.
2. Read through the dialogue, having students repeat the new vocabulary and practice in pairs.
3. Have pairs of students demonstrate their ability by reading the dialogue aloud.
4. Have students guess who the intended discourse participants might be and volunteer information on the style and register of the discourse (and how it differed from the one they worked with the day before).
5. Have the students guess the meaning of the new vocabulary in context. For example:

continued

Caveats and Options

1. Write half the conversation and have students work in pairs to come up with a matching half so that style and register differences as well as awareness of surrounding discourse become much more apparent.

2. Point out why the discourse did or did not work and have students judge the appropriateness of their peers' conversations. If there is a problem, students can offer explanations or suggestions for improvements.

Contributor

Gina Crocetti completed her MA in TESOL at Portland State University in 1992 while teaching in a preliteracy program she designed for St. Vincent Hospital. She currently teaches EFL at the UAE University in the United Arab Emirates.

Student-Centered Production

Levels
Intermediate

Aims
Develop responsibility
for learning and
production
Discern meaning
through context and
sentence structure

Class Time
1½ hours

Preparation Time
None

Resources
Chalkboard and chalk
Paper and pencil
Dictionaries

This task moves the focus from the teacher to the students. Using a central theme and their background schemata, they develop a dialogue which can be performed in class and is expressly designed to communicate meaning and fluency. The teacher acts as a facilitator rather than an instructor to inspire and motivate the students. This lesson is especially helpful for students who are quiet and lack confidence in their speaking abilities. By working in small chunks, building up the topic to a manageable level, and drawing on their background knowledge it shows the students how much they actually know.

Procedure

1. Have the students choose a topic (e.g., weather, greetings, hobbies).
2. Write two or three key words on the board.
3. Ask for suggestions from the students and write several on the board as the students write in their books.
4. From each of these key words, ask for two or three words or phrases that relate to them and write them down (e.g., for the key word *weather,* one student may offer "It's cold today, isn't it?"). For 10 key words, the students should produce 25–30 more connecting words or phrases.
5. Ask the students to write a plan for their dialogue (i.e., a rough outline, a rationale for what they want to say).
6. Circulate, helping students articulate what they want to say. (Most students will want to make notes or be writing their outline, but the teacher can help to make their ideas clear to the listener.)
7. If the students are not forthcoming with ideas or inspiration, offer suggestions to help them find some direction.

8. When they finish this, have the students confer with their partners, and check each other's work to confirm that main ideas are in place, and they understand the topic. The students are then ready to start their dialogues.

9. Have one student start by stating the scenario or situation, for example, "I spoke to the bus driver" or "My friend was waiting 2 hours," and opposite, write the actual speech quotation. (The students may also draw pictures and explain the pictures to their partner or teacher.)

10. Finally, with the culmination of the schematic mapping, word generation exercises, schemata building and written plans, ask the students to develop a polished dialogue, concentrating on coherence and fluency.

Caveats and Options

1. If there is time, have the students act out the dialogue in pairs or triads for the class, using correct intonation and props where necessary.

2. Grade the students or advise them on grammatical points or verbal skills as required.

3. You may include some or all of these exercises in one lesson, but the exercise is designed to be an interactive skills development task which calls on the students to be responsible for their own learning and make the class student centered. The students cooperate with each other to develop the dialogue and increase vocabulary.

Contributors

George Isted is Professor in the English and American Studies Department, and Paul Hackshaw is Lecturer in the same department, at Shitennoji International Buddhist University in Osaka, Japan.

Cassette DJs

Levels
Intermediate +

Aims
Experience a simulated
radio station as a way to
learn English

Class Time
Variable

Preparation Time
None

Resources
Recording equipment
(capable of recording
from one source to a
cassette)
Microphone for
recording DJ's voice

In this activity, students record simulated radio programs onto audiotape. Programs can have any content students choose (e.g., discussion, music, weather and traffic reports, advertising). The activity helps students be creative and relaxed while acting out the parts of radio announcers.

Procedure

1. Divide students into small groups and have them write a short prospectus for a radio program.
2. Have students decide who will play the different roles in the program.
3. Have groups prepare any weather or traffic reports, advertisements, or other prepared speech that will be use on their cassettes.
4. Have groups record their programs. Any groups whose program includes music should bring in music they like from their own collections.
5. Play the cassettes in the school cafeteria during lunchtime, or put them into a listening library for anyone to borrow.

Caveats and Options

1. The DJ's role and speech can be either planned or unplanned, depending on the level of your students.
2. The various groups' radio programs can be played for the entire class.

Contributor

Kenny Harsch is Director of English Education at Kobe YMCA College in Japan. He is interested in students developing uses for English, learner autonomy, and student-centered curriculum development. This activity was adapted from an idea by Ayumi Matsunaga at Kobe YMCA College.

A Cocktail Party

Levels
High intermediate +

Aims
Practice conversation in
an unstructured
environment
Improve and refine
fluency

Class Time
45–90 minutes

Preparation Time
15 minutes

Resources
Beverages, glasses, and
beverage trays

Finding speaking exercises to challenge advanced students often requires a lot of creativity. At the college level, students may find exercises in ESOL books babyish, uninteresting, or boring. Parties, however, are something students can relate to. This game simulates a real-life atmosphere that students are familiar with, and it has as its premise something young adults may find exciting, interesting, and worth practicing in a foreign language: socializing and meeting new people at parties. Students become so involved in the tasks of finding their designated partner and avoiding giving away their own identity that they hardly have time to worry about the real task: speaking English. It is one of those rare situations in which even the quietest student will surprise you with enthusiasm and a hidden talkative nature.

Procedure

1. Create a set of identity cards (see Appendix below).
2. Put one pair of cards in a hat (or envelope) for each pair of students present.
3. Have students pick an "identity" out of the hat and commit their identity to memory. Have students take a few minutes to think up a name for themselves and a short life history based on what is written on the card. Start the party by passing around drinks. Encourage introductions.
4. After the party starts, tell students to find their "partner" by asking questions to uncover the other student's identity.
5. Have students try to avoid answering questions directly so that they can avoid being identified for as long as possible.
6. In the name of improving English fluency, you can act as the host or hostess and break up the groups or pairs that form throughout the

party to extend the time needed to find partners. (You can say things like "Oh, darling, what's your name? Let me introduce you to so and so!")

7. After being identified, have the students sit down and continue their conversations in character.
8. Working with the partner, have the students write a short dialogue in line with the identity they've developed at the party.
9. Help the students with language problems that arise.

Caveats and Options

1. Use real glasses, beverages (whether alcoholic or not) and trays. Props such as these add to the fun of the game and add the touch of reality often needed to make games or exercises like this work.
2. Add a new dimension to the game by having students pick an emotion card, for example, love, despair, euphoria, boredom, or anguish. This emotion must be present in the dialogue in some way. Have students act out the dialogues in front of the class or from their seats.
3. When working with students who have trouble developing an unstructured dialogue, eliminate the emotion card and have them focus on a few specific tasks (e.g., introducing and getting to know their partner).
4. I found problems arose when students became so caught up with figuring out exactly when Ronald Reagan was elected or how old Nancy Reagan was that they gave up and wanted to pick a new identity. On the other hand, with jobs or personal relationships, students had trouble becoming creative enough to find a personality to match their identity.

References and Further Reading

Behma, H. (1985). *Miteinander Reden Lernen-Sprechspiele im Unterricht*. Munich, Germany: Iudicium Verlag GmbH.

Appendix: Creating Identity Cards

1. Make the identity cards unusual and interesting, with just enough information to stimulate students' imagination and make it difficult for them to know who their partner is. Adding adjectives to the identity can give an interesting twist to the game.
2. One set of sample pairs includes:
   - retired football player (famous in his time)
     up and coming football quarterback (young and inexperienced)
   - glutton
     gourmet cook
   - very nice looking, conceited lifeguard
     somebody who recently almost drowned
   - devout vegetarian
     owner of a chain of meat markets
   - psychoanalyst who psychoanalyzes everybody
     person in need of therapy
   - attractive professor
     student who regularly falls in love with professors
   - painter's nude model
     indecent, obscene painter
   - unfaithful husband
     faithful wife
   - busy doctor
     hypochondriac
   - reformed convict
     tough chief of police
3. Put one description from each pair on a card.
4. Also use famous pairs, different jobs or personal relationships (e.g., President and Mrs. Reagan, mother-daughter, trainer-soccer player).

Contributor

Rachel Baron Lester has taught EFL in Germany at high school, in college, and in adult education programs. She currently teaches EFL and American Culture at the University of Munich.

Drumming for Fluency

Levels
Beginning

Aims
Respond quickly in
English without
translating

Class Time
30 minutes

Preparation Time
30–60 minutes

Resources
Drum or other
percussion instrument
Pictures to elicit key
phrases
Chalkboard and chalk

Language flows more easily when a speaker is not preoccupied with accuracy. This activity creates a playful atmosphere in which students are free to experiment with different rhythms, speeds, and ways of saying the same phrases. Students access descriptive phrases from memory and reproduce them in a communicative dialogue while their attention is fixed on a drum and on each other's efforts to stay with the beat. Students are further encouraged to drop their guard as new talents and behaviors emerge with the drumbeat. Furthermore, they often remember and learn to appreciate the drumming traditions of their own countries.

Procedure

1. Prepare pictures to elicit key phrases for study and create a communicative dialogue with two characters using some of the phrases recently taught in class.
2. Arrange the students' chairs in a semicircle or U-shape and divide the class into two groups.
3. Place the pictures in front of the class and write the dialogue on the board so all the students can read it.
4. Have Group A and Group B read and practice the dialogue out loud in unison.
5. Once everyone is involved in the practice, discretely pull out the drum and start beating it lightly, trying to integrate the beat into the dialogue. (At first students are surprised, but eventually they get used to it. As the drumbeat grows louder they begin to synchronize their dialogue with it.)
6. You may find it necessary to model the activity with the following example (the ~ symbol denotes a drumbeat):

   - Group A: I ca~n't come to sch~ool.

- Group B: Why ca~n't you come to sch~ool?
- Group A: Beca~use I have a he~adache.
- Group B: Th~at's too b~ad.

7. Vary the speed as needed to challenge the students, and vary the key phrases to be inserted in the dialogue by pointing to the different pictures placed in front of the class (e.g., for the sample dialogue above, point to the pictures of a person with a toothache, stomachache, earache, backache).

8. Constantly move from one picture to another to keep the language flowing and to make it difficult for students to think in their L1 before responding in English.

9. When the students become comfortable with the activity, invoke the African oral tradition of the village drummer: Walk around the room beating the drum as students chant the dialogue and stop in front of one student who takes the part of Group A in the dialogue while the rest of the class takes Part B. (Choose only those students who are confident enough to lead in this way.)

10. Change the key phrases in the dialogue by walking back to the picture in the process and continue choosing leaders from the class until all students have practiced all the key phrases.

Caveats and Options

1. Have students practice a variety of linguistic items embedded in the dialogue (e.g., *can* vs. *can't*; *I have* vs. *he has*).

2. Individual students can play the drum and create their own rhythms.

3. The oral tradition can be further simulated by having students stand up in a circle with the drummer the center.

4. It is interesting how the drum, traditionally a sacred instrument, can create such a comical atmosphere in the classroom. Make sure that this atmosphere doesn't predominate and undermine the objective at hand. Have fun and have the students recognize how their fluency has improved at the end of the activity.

Contributor

Kaye Marshall began her teaching career as a Peace Corps volunteer in Niger, West Africa, followed by 4 years with a refugee program in Boston, Massachusetts. She is currently living in Japan.

Cafe Bianco

Levels
Any

Aims
Converse while using
new vocabulary
Develop restaurant
etiquette

Class Time
1–2 hours

Preparation Time
30 minutes

Resources
Menus, place settings,
napkins, tablecloths,
candles
Vocabulary Worksheet
(see Appendix below)

Role play is a highly effective method of improving conversational skills. This lesson utilizes a restaurant scenario to promote interaction between students in a familiar situation and introduce some practical aspects of restaurant dining.

Procedure

1. Using the props, set the scene and explain and model the characters of hostess/host, server, customers, and manager.
2. Pass out Vocabulary Worksheet (see Appendix below) to students and discuss concepts and new expressions (e.g., tipping). Vocabulary can be added or subtracted according to the level of the students.
3. Divide the class into small groups (based on the number of characters in the role play) and have them choose one of the scenarios suggested by the teacher (e.g., breakfast; lunch; dinner; Sunday brunch; customer forgets wallet; wedding rehearsal dinner; anniversary; unsatisfied customers; blind date; double date; marriage proposal).
4. Have students discuss and create a dialogue for presentation before the class.

Caveats and Options

1. Filming and viewing these presentations can be exciting and revealing for the learners and teacher.
2. Follow up the activity by going to a restaurant together.

Appendix: Vocabulary Worksheet

Vocabulary Words

Drinks: soda, iced tea, lemonade, milk, water, tea, coffee
Courses: appetizers, main course, and dessert
Utensils: fork, spoon, knife, steak knife, butter knife
Condiments: salt, pepper, sugar, spices, mustard, ketchup, mayonnaise
Dressings: italian, blue cheese, french, honey mustard, oil and vinegar
Soups: clam chowder, noodle soup, cream of broccoli, vegetable
Meat prepared: rare, medium rare, medium, medium well, well done
Sauces: tartar sauce, steak sauce, hot sauce, barbecue sauce, soy sauce
Check: food, drinks, tax, tip

Common Expressions

Party of (number). Smoking or nonsmoking?
Are you ready to order?
I'd like to order _____ .
How would you like your steak done?
What kind of dressing would you like on your salad?
Please pass the _____ .
Would you like some dessert or coffee?
May we have the check please?
Was everything all right?
Thank you and please come again.

Contributor

Kathleen McNally teaches at ELS Language Center, San Diego, California in the United States. She has taught elementary and adult levels of ESL and has presented papers at many conferences.

The Fluency Fair

Levels
Intermediate +

Aims
Give short talks
Improve fluency and
accuracy

Class Time
1½–2 hours

Preparation Time
30 minutes

Resources
Classroom with walking
space
Short articles on new
products, including
pictures

In many fluency activities involving problem solving or discussion, students have the opportunity to react in a natural, communicative manner. However, because of the flow of topics, students may rarely get the chance to improve their performance by trying to get the same message across twice. A fair or exhibition, where people walk around and stop to listen to different short presentations, gives students a chance to give the same talk to the listeners several times in a row. This task can improve both fluency and accuracy.

Procedure

1. Paste an article on one side of note cards or paper and the picture of the new product on the other side. (Advertisements and articles from back issues of *Newsweek, Time,* or business journals are ideal.)
2. Set the stage for the fair by announcing that everyone has a large sum of money (e.g., $500,000) to invest in a new product.
3. Have the class brainstorm a list of criteria that make new products particularly promising or attractive and write the list on the board.
4. Pair off the students and give each pair a different article/picture card.
5. Have the pairs of students read and discuss the information about the product and prepare a short, persuasive presentation for the class. (They can make notes, but they should not write out their talk word for word.)
6. Have students arrange themselves into "booths" for the product fair, where they (as inventors or companies) will present their products to potential investors who will walk around the fair to listen and invest their money.

7. One student from each pair remains at the booth and prepares for interested investors, and the other student from the pair takes on the investor role, visiting each booth at the fair.

8. Have the investors listen to the presentations, ask questions, and make notes about which product they will invest in and why.

9. Once each investor has had an opportunity to listen to each presentation, have the pairs switch roles and go through the entire process of the exhibition again.

10. After each student has taken both roles, have the students comment on and discuss their investment intentions with the whole class or in small groups.

Caveats and Options

1. I generally do very little correcting during the activity, as students seem to become more accurate in the course of the multiple presentations. You can provide a few common presentation phrases as a model to build students' confidence.

2. Timing can be tricky, and I find most of my attention is taken up with supplying the odd word and making sure investors circulate frequently so that each presenter has a listener.

3. With larger classes, presentation and products can be shared by small groups or the activity can be extended over two class periods.

4. The fair/exhibition format is useful with other topics (e.g., presenting and explaining optical illusions, logic puzzles, or grammar points). Instead of investing money profitably, students are motivated to listen to the other presentations because they have questions to answer, problems to solve, or sentences to correct.

Contributor

Heather Murray teaches English for Academic Purposes and EFL Methodology at the University of Bern in Switzerland.

Disc Jockey Spins a Tune

Levels
Beginning–intermediate

Aims
Gain confidence in
speaking English in a
nonthreatening
environment

Class Time
5 minutes/learner

Preparation Time
5–10 minutes

Resources
Song tape
Audiotape recorder

Many beginning and intermediate learners are shy to use the spoken language. Speaking spontaneously to the class makes them even more nervous. This activity provides students with the opportunity to prepare notes and speak purposefully to a radio audience of the teacher and classmates. As learners build confidence through this activity, they can move toward less controlled face-to-face communication.

Procedure

1. Set the scene by telling students to imagine they are disc jockeys (DJs) at a radio station and they will be able to introduce their favorite song to the audience (class) during the next lesson. (You may want to demonstrate the procedures below.)
2. Have students choose a song they like and record it.
3. Have students make notes about the song to use while introducing it to classmates. Have them include information about the title of the song, the author, the singer, the story of the song, and why it is their favorite (e.g., the melody, lyrics, writer, singer, or the arrangement).
4. Have students rehearse their DJ introduction to their favorite song at home until they feel comfortable with their voices.
5. Have students bring their tapes and notes to the next lesson.
6. Have the class close their eyes and tune in as each student introduces the song and plays the tape for the class in a radio station role play.

Caveats and Options

For bigger classes, have learners work in groups of five.

- Have each group discuss and choose a song. Then have each student in the group take individual notes and rehearse.
- Make sure one person from each group tapes the song and brings it to the next lesson.

- Randomly select one from each group to be the disc jockey. (All have prepared and discussed the songs in small groups for speaking practice in a nonthreatening environment.)

Contributor

Wai-king Tsang is Lecturer at the English Department at City Polytechnic of Hong Kong. She holds an MA in ESL from the University of Hawaii at Manoa.

Interactive Dialogue Practice

Levels
Beginning–intermediate

Aims
Practice dialogues
without reading from or
memorizing the text
Use appropriate body
language and facial
expressions

Class Time
Variable

Preparation Time
None

Resources
Textbook with (or
handouts) of a dialogue
Audiotape of the
dialogue

Almost all conversation textbooks include dialogues, which most teachers have their students practice. To avoid what is often a dead reading of the text, with little interaction between the partners, this activity has student helpers feed the lines to performers who repeat them. Performers, thus freed from either concentrating on reading or memory overload, are encouraged to look at their partners and to use appropriate intonation, facial expressions, and gestures. This activity is an intermediate step toward more natural conversation.

Procedure

1. Divide the class into groups (four students each is preferable).
2. Have the class listen to a recording of the dialogue (or demonstrate it yourself).
3. Have students mark the text for phrasing, stress, and intonation, as you demonstrate the body language and show how the helpers can be effective prompters by feeding the performers phrases of a suitable length for repetition.
4. Have two students take the role of the helpers, sit behind the performers, and whisper the lines of the dialogue to them (have the performers close their books and face their partners in the dialogue).
5. Have the performers repeat the lines of the dialogue to their partner, trying to communicate the meaning, using appropriate body language. (If the performers do not understand the lines, they can ask the helpers to repeat them.)
6. Have the helpers and performers switch roles and do the dialogue again.

7. As students become familiar with the dialogue, have performers try to say the lines without being prompted, turning to the helpers only when necessary.

Caveats and Options

1. As a follow-up activity, one or two groups can perform in front of the whole class.
2. Students with enough ability and confidence can try to vary the dialogue by substituting different words and expressions.

Contributor

Roberta A. Welch has been an EFL teacher for 20 years and is currently teaching at Tokyo Women's College in Japan. She received her MA in TESOL from Temple University Japan.

◆ Games for Speaking
Talking With Tangrams

Levels
Any

Aims
Learn vocabulary and
functions related to
size, color, location, and
direction
Reinforce mastery of
commands
Think creatively

Class Time
Variable

Preparation Time
10 minutes

Resources
Colored construction
paper and scissors or
colored tiles (wood or
plastic) of various
shapes

Tangrams are an enjoyable and versatile teaching tool and can be used to create as many classroom activities as there are possible shapes from the puzzle pieces. This activity creates an atmosphere of cooperation and teamwork in which learners must use their language resources to communicate information vital to the completion of an information gap task with a partner. In addition, the puzzlelike aspects of the task are motivating and enjoyable.

Procedure

1. Prepare, or have students prepare, seven Tangram pieces by outlining originals on paper (preferably colored paper) and then cutting them out (see below). One set can be used for the whole class or multiple sets can be created for groups of learners.

Tangrams 1

2. Tell the students the following story:
   A long time ago in China, a potter named Tan dropped a ceramic tile that broke into seven pieces. While attempting to reconstruct the tile, the potter noticed that the seven pieces of tile (now called *Tangrams* after the potter) could be made into all kinds of interesting forms: animals, people, buildings, symbols, and abstract shapes.

3. Have learners, in pairs or other groups, sit across the table or desk facing each other, and place the tiles (made of construction paper) in front of the student(s) on one side of the table with the solution (see below) to the puzzle in front of the student(s) on the other side of the table. (Make sure the solution is kept hidden from the sight of those solving the puzzle.)

Solution

Tangrams 2

4. Have the student(s) with the solution use size, color, direction, and location words and phrases to help the other student(s) construct the correct figure. (For example, to create the rabbitlike figure illustrated below, students could use phrases describing where to place which shape, what direction it should face, what sides should touch . . .).

Solution

Tangrams 3

5. Let the constructors ask any questions they'd like, but don't let students with the solution use their bodies in any way, or speak in their L1 when giving instructions. (For instance, in response to the question, "Should I put the big triangle on top or underneath?" a student could say, "You may move the red triangle to the left, near the middle of the small green triangle.")

6. When the Tangram is complete, have the student(s) change positions. (You may choose to make this task competitive.)

Caveats and Options

1. Provide a group with one of the filled-in pictures (see above) and have the group work together to discover how the form was constructed.
2. Instead of providing students with solutions, it can be interesting and enjoyable for them to play with the tiles and come up with figures of their own. (Stipulate that the object must be recognizable and that the tiles may not overlap.) Have the team outline the figure they've created on a blank piece of paper and challenge the other teams to construct the object.
3. For a writing segment, have students develop a new form and write the instructions for their partner, or have students write a story about a design and how it came to be. (The story can be the basis for class discussion.)
4. For vocabulary practice, present students with vocabulary words and have them create the nearest approximation of the new word or something that symbolizes it.
5. Plastic tiles are also available commercially under such names as *Tangoes*.

References and Further Reading

For further information about Tangrams, see books such as J. Effers' *Tangram: The ancient Chinese shapes game* (Penguin).

Contributor

J. Egbert is completing her PhD at the University of Arizona and teaches ESL at Palomar College in San Marcos, California in the United States.

Location Question Race

Levels
High
beginning–intermediate

Aims
Generate as many
questions as possible
about the location of a
certain item without
focusing on accuracy

Class Time
15 minutes

Preparation Time
5 minutes

Resources
Question Worksheet
(see Appendix below)

Yes-no questions are a basic component of speaking. However, for speaking purposes, this question pattern is usually taught with traditional exercises such as drills or other exercises devoid of real meaning. This activity makes students speak and listen, and what they say and hear makes a difference in completing the task successfully. As with any good game, there is also an element of luck involved.

Procedure

1. Give each student a worksheet.
2. Have students make five original sentences by putting a check mark in the box by one part in A and one part in B. (So, for each sentence, there are 16 possible combinations.)
3. Have students work in pairs to guess their partner's choices. They must ask questions. For example, in Number 1, they ask questions about their partner's cat. Student A will begin: "Is your cat under the chair?" If the answer is no, Student B can ask a question. If the answer is yes, Student A can continue to ask questions.
4. When a student knows the first part, he or she then asks about the second part. For example, in Number 1, if the cat is on the TV, the student will then ask "Is your cat on the TV near the front door?" If the answer is no, it is the other student's turn.

continued

90

Appendix: Question Worksheet

	Column A	Column B
1. My cat is	❏ under the chair ❏ on the chair ❏ on the rug ❏ on the TV	❏ near the front door ❏ in the bedroom ❏ by the coffee table ❏ in the living room
2. His shoes are	❏ on the floor ❏ on the chair ❏ on the table ❏ on the TV	❏ in the kitchen ❏ in the living room ❏ in the dining room ❏ in his bedroom
3. The book is	❏ in a box ❏ in an envelope ❏ in a bag ❏ on the floor	❏ under my bed ❏ in the closet ❏ by the door ❏ next to the sofa
4. The map is	❏ on the left wall ❏ on the right wall ❏ on a desk ❏ in a large envelope	❏ in the class ❏ in the office ❏ at the bank ❏ in her room
5. The coins are	❏ in a box ❏ in a bag ❏ in a safe ❏ in an envelope	❏ under my bed ❏ in the kitchen ❏ at the bank ❏ in the cabinet

From *Talking A Lot* by Keith S. Folse, published by the University of Michigan Press. Copyright by the University of Michigan, 1993. Used with permission.

Contributor

Keith S. Folse has taught in the United States, Saudi Arabia, Malaysia, and Japan. He is the author of several ESL textbooks.

Singing Hide-and-Seek

Levels
Beginning –
intermediate; children

Aims
Learn greetings rituals
in the context of a
game

Class Time
7 minutes for small
group

Preparation Time
None

Resources
Tune to the children's
song, "Where Is
Thumbkin?"

This activity gives children a chance to learn and use greetings without consciously being aware that they are doing so. As well, there is a cultural element present in that the children are indirectly learning about aspects of the game of hide-and-seek. This routine can be varied through alternative responses and by eventually interchanging roles between the teacher and one of the students. This activity is a good way to begin or end a lesson, depending on what else needs to be accomplished that day and whether the children need a chance to relax and move around before or after a more stationary activity.

Procedure

1. Assume the "seeker" role of hide-and-seek for the first few times the game is played, and tell the children to go and hide while you count to 15. (Other students can accompany newer students to hiding places.)
2. After counting aloud to 15, start singing "Where is Ayumi? Where is Ayumi?" (or any of the children's names) to the tune of "Where is Thumbkin?"
3. Have the children pop up from the hiding place when they hear their name called, and sing (or say in rhythm) "Here I am! Here I am!" (You can sing for the children who are still reluctant.)
4. While stretching out your hand, sing "How are you today, miss (or sir)?"
5. Have the child reply, "Very well (fine), I thank you" and shake hands.
6. Then sing "Run away! Run away!" and have the child run off.
7. Repeat this with each student in the class.

Caveats and Options

1. After the students have grown accustomed to the song and routine, you can talk to them about how they could change their response to "How are you today, miss (sir)?" to reflect how they really are feeling.
2. Also, you can become one of the "hiders," and a student can be a "seeker."
3. One possible shortcoming of this activity is that it resembles a substitution drill and perhaps has the potential of being memorized rather than being a communicative process. However, this aside, it is the most requested activity by kindergarterners who thoroughly love the repetition and the hiding aspect of it. As well, it is a progressive activity where increasing proficiency allows for more oral participation, without eliminating still silent students from joining in and enjoying themselves.

Contributor

Randi Freeman taught ESOL in Sweden. She now teaches in an elementary school in California, while pursuing an MA in TESOL at Monterey Institute of International Studies in the United States.

English Baseball

Levels
Any

Aims
Enjoy using English in a
familiar game situation
Practice negotiating
meaning as a listening
skill
Become aware of
pronunciation problems

Class Time
Variable

Preparation Time
1 hour

Resources
Chalkboard and chalk
Envelope
Paper for creating
question cards

ESOL students are often eager to learn about sports and games in their language and culture of study. This activity uses a question-and-answer format to help learners develop speaking skills while learning about the sport of baseball.

Procedure

1. Create question cards (pitches) using the guidelines in the Appendix.
2. Divide the class into two teams and arrange the room into a makeshift baseball diamond.
3. Explain to the students that this activity is question and answer practice using the game of baseball. A pitcher from one team will ask a question to a batter from the other team. If the batter can answer the question, it is a hit (based on the value on the question card). Teams compete for home runs.
4. Have each team choose its batting order (which is also its pitching order).
5. Set up a scoreboard on the chalkboard and designate a scorekeeper.
6. The first member of the pitching team draws a question pitch from the envelope and asks it to the respondent/batter on the other team. If the batter answers the question satisfactorily, the student moves to the appropriate base designated by the difficulty level of the question. If the batter fails to answer the question satisfactorily, the student is out. Three outs end the batting team's half of the inning. (The pitcher should announce the correct answer for each out.)
7. Continue play until nine innings are finished (with both teams getting a turn at bat in each inning).
8. Tally the score and declare a winner.

Caveats and Options

1. This activity works best if the students and teacher already understand baseball. For a more intricate game of baseball, add other rules.
2. Count a "strike" against the batter if the student doesn't understand the question, but can say something in English to help himself or herself (e.g., if she asks the pitcher or teacher what an unknown vocabulary word means, asks for clarification or repetition). The batter is allowed to do this twice; three strikes equal an out.
3. If a pitcher's reading of a question is incoherent (e.g., due to poor pronunciation), the batter can appeal to the umpire (teacher). If the umpire agrees, the pitch counts as a *ball.* Four balls is a *walk* and the batter takes first base.
4. If the pitcher asks an unsuitable question (e.g., "What is my favorite color?"), the batter can appeal to the umpire. If the umpire agrees that the question is impossible to answer, the question is considered a *balk,* and the batter takes first base.
5. If there is a runner on base, and a batter feels he or she cannot answer a question, the student can ask the runner on base to answer. If the runner answers satisfactorily the batter is out, but the runner can advance one base (a *sacrifice*). If the runner doesn't answer satisfactorily, both batter and runner are out (a *double play*).
6. This game could probably be adopted to cricket or other sports.

Appendix: Creating Pitches for English Baseball

1. An envelope of "pitches" should include cards shaped like baseballs using trivia questions ranging in difficulty with the designations 1-single, 2-double, 3-triple, and H-home run.
2. Sample pitch cards:

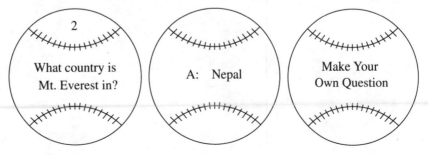

3. The number and baseball term on the card indicates the difficulty of the question (e.g., 1-single questions are the easiest).

4. The answer to the trivia questions (or any topic questions) should be on the back of the cards. (For some questions the answer could vary according to the batter and a hit is to be awarded based on the relevance of the answer.)

5. Create Make Your Own Question cards that require the pitcher in the game to create a question for the batter. Any question that is possible for the batter to answer is allowable, but questions such as "What is my favorite color?" would not be a fair ball. (The value of the question depends on the difficulty and is up to the discretion of the umpire, who is usually the teacher.)

Contributors

Kenny Harsch and Randy Smith teach and develop materials at the Kobe YMCA College in Japan. This activity was adapted from an idea by Troy Miller at Kobe YMCA Language Center.

Paraphrasing Races

Levels
Intermediate–advanced

Aims
Practice paraphrasing
Become aware of
several ways to say the
same thing

Class Time
15–30 minutes

Preparation Time
10 minutes

Resources
Sentences for students
to paraphrase

Paraphrasing can be a useful tool in conversation for explaining or clarifying the meaning of something without embarrassing yourself or anyone else in the process. Paraphrasing Races allows students the freedom to play with language in groups and create new sentences without the pressure of a real conversation. Mistakes can actually be turned into great learning experiences.

Procedure

1. Divide students into teams of two to five people.
2. Show the students examples of paraphrasing (e.g., *He went to the zoo*; *He went to a place that has animals in cages*; *He didn't go to a movie* [unacceptable for above sentences]).
3. Read a sentence (or write it on the board), and have the students come up with as many rephrasings as they can in 3 minutes.
4. At the end of 3 minutes, ask each group to read aloud their paraphrases. Give one point to each team for each acceptable paraphrase they generate.
5. Repeat Steps 3 and 4 for as many sentences as you want.
6. After all the sentences are finished, tally the total points for each team and declare a winner.

Caveats and Options

1. Point out to the students that paraphrases can be syntactically generated by using an alternative word order (e.g., active vs. passive sentences) and lexically generated (by using synonyms).
2. You can use paraphrases to illustrate register difference. For example, *He died,* and *He passed away* and *He kicked the bucket* all have the same referential meaning, but their registers vary.

3. Be sure to discuss the extent of paraphrasing and synthesis needed to avoid plagiarizing.

Contributor

Kenny Harsch is Director of English Education at Kobe YMCA College in Japan. He is interested in students developing uses for English, learner autonomy, and student-centered curriculum development.

Partners

Levels
Any

Aims
Get to know classmates
better
Practice asking and
answering questions

Class Time
15 minutes/round

Preparation Time
Variable

Resources
Game show realia (e.g.,
microphone and music)

Partners use the format of an exciting game show and take the typical classroom icebreaker activity to another realm. When students pretend they are participants in a game show, they tend to get so involved that they forget their inhibitions about speaking.

Procedure

1. Pair off students with an unfamiliar partner.
2. Give partners 3–5 minutes to talk together with instructions to try and find out as much as possible about each other.
3. Give students examples of questions and answers they can create. (Prepare a list of suggested questions for low-level or extremely quiet classes.)
4. To begin the game, have four students and their partners sit in front of the class. (The other students are the audience and will take their turns as contestants later.)
5. Have students in the audience keep track of how many of the contestants' answers match their partners' answers.
6. Act as the master of ceremonies (MC) and ask the partners sitting on the right to leave the room.
7. Ask each remaining partner three questions, in order, about the partner who has left the room (e.g., *How long has your partner lived in this city?*).
8. Have the partners come back into the classroom and take their places.
9. One by one, ask the students who were outside the classroom the same questions their partners have just answered. If the answers match, the pair gets five points.

99

10. Repeat the procedure with the partners sitting on the left side, or if the class is large move on to new sets of partners. The pair with the most points at the end of the game wins.

Caveats and Options

To ensure that this activity is as successful as possible, here are some helpful hints for creating a festive game show atmosphere:
- The MC should really ham it up.
- Make use of realia like a microphone and of sound affects like music and buzzers.
- Award prizes (e.g., hold up a picture of a palm tree and say, "Congratulations! You have just won a trip to Hawaii! You can leave anytime you have enough money!")

Contributors

Sally La Luzerne-Oi has taught in Mexico, Venezuela, Portugal, Japan, and is currently an instructor at Hawaii Pacific University in the United States. Cindy McKeag Tsukamoto has been teaching for about 10 years and is currently Assistant Professor of ESL at Roosevelt University, Chicago, Illinois, in the United States.

Word Ping Pong

Levels
High beginning–
intermediate

Aims
Practice terminal word
sound recognition and
production

Class Time
5–10 minutes

Preparation Time
None

Resources
Chalkboard or
whiteboard and pens

In this activity, students focus on the pronunciation of sounds within words. Students have to produce words beginning with the last sound of a preceding word. The analogy is with playing the game of ping pong, only instead of hitting a ball to each other, the students are "serving" and "returning" words.

Student 1:	*carpet*
Student 2:		*tall*
Student 1:			*light*
Student 2:				*top*
Student 1:					*print*
Student 2:						*television*

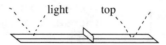

A student loses the game if he cannot think of a return word within 5 seconds or if the returning word begins with the wrong sound.

Procedure

1. Elicit the meaning of ping pong through using mime, pictures, or explanation.
2. Tell the class that they are going to play word ping pong.
3. Draw two stickmen facing each other, one at either end of the chalkboard or whiteboard, each holding a ping pong paddle.
4. Draw large speech bubbles from each of the stickmen's mouths.
5. In one stickman's speech bubble, write the word *fast*.
6. Ask the class which sound the word *fast* ends with.

7. Write a word beginning with *t* in the other stickman's speech bubble, for example, *tap*.
8. Ask which sound the word *tap* ends with.
9. Then write a word beginning with *p*, for example, *picnic*, in the first stickman's speech bubble.
10. Further demonstrate the game with one of the more confident members of the class or with the whole class.
11. Put the students in pairs and invite them to play games of Word Ping Pong.

Caveats and Options

1. You may use any words in English, including names of people, places and products.
2. Don't allow dictionaries because this will slow the game down.
3. If words end with a silent *e,* the silent *e* is ignored. The responding word should begin with the last sound (i.e., the last phoneme) of the given word, for example, *wave,* followed by *very*.
4. Tell students the same word may not be used twice in any one game.
5. As a variation, the game may be played in a group of four as doubles.
6. Before the game, it may be useful to elicit a bank of words beginning with *y*.
7. Word Ping Pong is particularly useful with students who regularly omit final consonant sounds in their mother tongue (e.g., Cantonese, Mandarin, Japanese, Thai, Korean and Vietnamese speakers).
8. Word Ping Pong is a good ice breaker at the start of a class.
9. For lower levels, this procedure also works well as a follow-up spelling game.

Contributor

Dino Mahoney is Senior Lecturer in the English Department of the City Polytechnic of Hong Kong.

Toss and Tell Us

Levels
Low intermediate +

Aims
Answer content
questions about the real
world
Generate feedback on
peers' performance

Class Time
Variable

Preparation Time
None

Resources
Pair of dice
Roll of Dice sheet (see
Appendix below)

This activity accesses linguistic knowledge from memory in an oral mode and provides students with practice in reading short sentences aloud to the class. This practice is achieved through understanding and speaking in response to short directives covering a variety of subjects. Students who are not participating have an opportunity to learn information—for example, the answers to the short directives—so that when their turns come they will be able to answer fluently.

Procedure

1. Select a student at random to roll the dice.
2. Have that student roll the dice to obtain a number from the Roll of Dice sheet.
3. Then ask the student to choose a classmate, select Answers A, B, or C from the Roll of Dice sheet, and read it to the selected classmate.
4. The selected student responds. If the student cannot respond, have the first student read another one of the three items (A, B, or C).
5. If the student again cannot respond, read the third choice.
6. Should the student still not be able to respond, that student loses this turn. Have the first student roll again and select a new student to answer.
7. Have the selected student respond and then turn his/her back to the class.
8. Then have the class vote on the performance as follows: Thumb up = excellent; thumb horizontal = satisfactory; thumb down = needs improvement.
9. Count the tallies and report the scores orally to the selected classmate.

10. Have the student who rolled the dice pass them to the student who responded, who then selects another student at random and the activity continues.

Caveats and Options

1. Rather than giving an accurate count of thumb up/horizontal/down, the teacher (or other vote counter) can generalize: "Mostly satisfactory, a few excellents, and no thumbs down" and so forth.
2. Two students may be used instead of one to respond. This cooperative effort can add some variety to the answers and may speed up the responses if that is desired. For example, in response to: *Tell us what country you would like to visit and why,* the students may have different desires, and their different responses will provide added lexical items for listening practice.
3. Letting the students do all the work in an activity like this is desirable and allows you to observe carefully the students' performance and, where indicated, make brief notes for later use in counseling or tutoring an individual basis. Or, as is often the case, particular problems common to many or all students may surface, which you may wish to address later while working with the class.

Appendix: Roll of Dice Sheet

Roll the dice to obtain a number from 2 to 12. After the number has been determined, select Answer A, B, or C and read it to the student selected in a voice loud enough for all of the class to hear.

Roll of 2:
  a. Tell us who you think are the two most important people in the world today and explain why you think so.
  b. Tell us what your two favorite subjects in school are and explain why you like them.
  c. Tell us two things you like to do in your spare time.

Roll of 3:
  a. Tell us the name of the last movie you saw and if you liked it, tell us why.
  b. Tell us what country you would like to visit and why.
  c. Tell us, in detail, what you had for dinner last night.

Roll of 4:
  a. Tell us four things you like about yourself.
  b. Tell us one thing you don't like about yourself.
  c. Tell us the name of one item of clothing you would buy if someone gave you enough money to buy it and explain why.

Roll of 5:
  a. Tell us who is the tallest boy in the class. Prove your answer.
  b. Tell us what the weather is like today.
  c. Tell us your dog's name if you have one. If you don't have a dog, what would you name one if you did?

Roll of 6:
  a. Tell us the names of four grains that people eat.
  b. Tell us the names of four diseases.
  c. Tell us what size shoe you wear.

Roll of 7:
  a. Tell us what you have in your right front pants pocket if you are wearing trousers. If not, tell us what brand of toothpaste you use.
  b. Tell us what you think is the most serious problem facing the world today.
  c. Tell us how to get to the school cafeteria.

Roll of 8:
  a. Tell us whether most blood flows to the heart or from the heart.
  b. Tell us where your food goes after you swallow it.
  c. Tell us which you like better, cats or dogs, and give us your reasons.

Roll of 9:

a. Tell us who you would invite to go on a date with you if you could invite anybody in the world.

b. Tell us what ice cream is made of.

c. Tell us where the oldest trees in the world grow.

Roll of 10:

a. Tell us approximately how many people live in China.

b. Tell us three qualities you like in a person.

c. Tell us what your favorite dessert is and what it is made of.

Roll of 11:

a. Tell us what state in the United States has the most people.

b. Tell us the names of five different pieces of furniture.

c. Tell us the name of the largest mammal that lives in the ocean.

Roll of 12:

a. Tell us the name of one famous poet.

b. Tell us at what temperature water freezes in both centigrade and fahrenheit measurements.

c. Tell us which animal(s) provide(s) us with wool.

Contributor

Ted Plaister taught in the Department of ESL, University of Hawaii, for 24 years. He has also taught in Thailand, Japan, Micronesia, and American Samoa.

My Friends Call Me Ted

Levels
High beginning +

Aims
Learn relationship
between given names
and nicknames

Class Time

Variable

Preparation Time
1 hour

Resources
List of female and male
names with
corresponding
nicknames (see
Appendix below)
Two sets of index cards,
each set a different
color

Handling names with fluency in an L2 is a useful but seldom taught skill. This task involves being able to recall a person's nickname from the given name and vice versa. Speakers of languages other than English may have difficulty distinguishing between female and male names and may become confused when hearing both a given name and a nickname used. This exercise teaches them the pairings of common given names and nicknames in a gamelike environment.

Procedure

1. Put one name and its nickname on the same side of each card (one color card for male names and the other color for female names).
2. Give each female student and each male student a card of corresponding color.
3. Teach the following model orally to the class: *My given (or first) name is Theodore, but my friends call me Ted.* (When responding, students may choose either to use *given* or *first*.
4. Select a monitor and as each student generates a sentence (substituting the names on the card for Theodore-Ted), have the monitor write the names on the chalkboard under the appropriate columns: Given/First Name, Nickname.
5. Tell the students not to write down the names written on the chalkboard. As students say their sentences, there may be some significant mispronunciations of one or both of the names. If so, you should interrupt briefly to model the names.
6. After all the names have been put on the chalkboard, go over the pronunciation of the names quickly, but it is not necessary for the students to repeat the names in chorus.

7. Then put the students into small groups, with the size depending upon the number of students in the class.
8. Have the monitor erase the nicknames from the chalkboard, Group 1, Group 2, etc.
9. The monitor then calls on Group 1 as follows: "What is the nickname for Theodore?" The members of Group 1 decide among themselves what it is. If they get it correct, they receive one point. If they do not, the monitor goes to Group 2 and asks the same question. If they get it correct, they get another chance until they produce an incorrect answer. Play then moves to Group 3 and so forth until all nicknames have been supplied.
10. The group with the highest number of points wins.

Caveats and Options

1. If there is sufficient time, reverse the process and put the nicknames on the chalkboard and elicit the given/first names from the groups.
2. If the class is small, students may work as individuals rather than in groups.
3. A discussion may be held on the use of nicknames in other cultures including how nicknames are chosen or if they are used at all.
4. Point out to students that in English there is sometimes no relation between a person's given name and nickname, for example, *Skip* as the nickname for somebody named *Thomas,* instead of the expected *Tom*.

continued

Appendix:
Sample First/
Given Names:
Nicknames

Male	
Theodore	Ted
Frederick	Fred
Thomas	Tom
Samuel	Sam
Henry	Hank
Francis	Frank
Michael	Mike
Douglas	Doug
Robert	Bob/Rob
Edward	Ed/Ted
Philip	Phil
Richard	Dick/Rich
Harold	Harry
Arthur	Art
Donald	Don
Charles	Charley/Chuck
Clement	Clem
David	Dave
Everett	Ev
James	Jim/Jimmy
Manuel	Manny
Peter	Pete
Roger	Rog
Lawrence	Larry
Jerome	Jerry
Gregory	Greg
Terence	Terry
Vernon	Vern
Walter	Walt
Wallace	Wally
Stuart	Stu
Raymond	Ray
Nathaniel	Nat
Christopher	Chris
Patrick	Pat

Female	
Kathleen	Kathy
Elizabeth	Beth/Betty/Liz
Margaret	Peg/Peggy
Sally	Sal
Frances	Fran
Sarah	Sally
Christine	Chris
Catherine	Katy/Kit
Dorothy	Dot
Gwendolyn	Gwen
Jennifer	Jenny
Nancy	Nan
Penelope	Penny
Victoria	VIcky
Grace	Gracie
Sandra	Sandy
Melanie	Mel
Cassandra	Cassy
Virginia	Ginny
Rebecca	Becky
Gertrude	Gert
Abigail	Abby
Agnes	Aggie
Barbara	Babs/Barb
Beatrice	Bea
Beverly	Bev
Candace	Candy
Caroline	Carrie
Constance	Connie
Deborah	Debbie
Eleanor	Ellie
Florence	Flo
Mildred	Millie
Susan	Sue
Patricia	Pat/Patty

Contributor

Ted Plaister taught in the Department of ESL, University of Hawaii, for 24 years. He has also taught in Thailand, Japan, Micronesia, and American Samoa.

Speak Well and Win

Levels
Intermediate +

Aims
Practice impromptu
speaking in a gamelike
setting

Resources
Deck of playing cards
List of 52 speaking
activities (see Appendix
below)

Class Time
Variable

Preparation Time
None

This activity utilizes a standard deck of playing cards to distribute speaking tasks to students. Using randomly selected cards to distribute speaking tasks introduces a gamelike element and gives each student an equal chance of being assigned any of the tasks.

Procedure

1. Determine the order of play.
2. Seat students in a circle, or in rows. (If students are seated in rows, the player that has the turn should stand and face the others.)
3. Draw the top card from the deck and hand it to the first player. The player looks at the card and says, "I have the _____ of _____." (e.g., *I have the queen of hearts*). The student loses a turn if he or she makes an error.
4. Consult the List of 52 Speaking Activities (see Appendix) and tell the student what to do.
5. Have the student do the speaking activity from the list and have the other students vote on the performance (with their eyes closed, if you wish) as follows:

   - thumbs up = 5 points (Excellent)
   - thumbs in = 3 points (Good)
   - thumbs down = 1 point (So-so)

6. Suggest the following criteria for judging by explaining the meaning of these terms to the students: Poise; Use of language (quantity and quality); Information content; Interest.
7. Have the students open their eyes and judge their voting as follows:

   - majority of thumbs up = 5 points
   - some thumbs up and some thumbs in = 4 points

- majority of thumbs in = 3 points
- some thumbs in and some thumbs down = 2 points
- majority of thumbs down = 1 point

(The scoring is obviously not exact, and you will have to exercise judgment in determining the final score.)

8. Announce the score and have the score keeper mark the score for the individual as the play continues.

9. If a student draws the Joker, the student gets a chance at 10 points if she can recite "The Purple Cow" without error. If the recitation is not errorfree (you be the judge), the performance is scored the same as any other. (Provide each student with a copy of the poem and do some choral practice in advance of the game as a model.)

> The Purple Cow
> by Gelett Burgess
>
> I never saw a purple cow,
> I never hope to see one;
> But I can tell you anyhow,
> I'd rather see than be one.

10. The student with the highest number of points after all the cards have been played is the winner.

Caveats and Options

1. If you are working with a large group of students and have run through the entire deck of cards, shuffle the deck and continue the game. The chances of a student getting the same card again are very

slim. Should a student get the same card, bury the card in the deck and give that student another card.

2. It is not recommended that students be given the list of topics in advance and prepare to recite. If students are quietly rehearsing what they are going to say when it is their turn, they will not be listening carefully to the student who is talking.

3. Although 52 different topics have been provided for this game in the Appendix, you may wish to write some of your own to fit your particular students.

References and Further Reading

Burgess, G. (1961). *The purple cow and other nonsense*. New York: Dover.

Appendix: Speak Well and Win

♠ Spades

Ace	Name the fingers.
King	Describe the clothing of another student.
Queen	Describe an orange.
Jack	Say the first seven letters of the alphabet backwards.
Ten	Give the first names of all members of your group.
Nine	Describe the room in which this game is being played.
Eight	Describe what you had for lunch yesterday.
Seven	Name the colors of the rainbow.
Six	Ask another player five questions.
Five	Describe your family.
Four	Tell why you are studying English.
Three	Say what you would do if you found $10,000 in cash.
Two	Describe your ideal mate.

♥ Hearts

Ace	Tell the most frightening experience you've ever had.
King	Describe the neighborhood where you live back home.
Queen	Which dead person do you admire the most?
Jack	Which living person do you admire the most?

Ten	Describe the best time you've ever had in your life.
Nine	Tell one thing you'd like to change in your country.
Eight	Tell how to make something.
Seven	Explain the difference between *weather* and *climate*.
Six	Tell about the most serious illness you've ever had.
Five	Tell what kind of work you want to do for a living.
Four	Name your favorite spectator sport and tell why you like it.
Three	Name your favorite television program and tell why you like it.
Two	Tell how many children you would like to have, what sexes they would be, and the reason for your choices.

♦ Diamonds

Ace	Compose a telegram to be sent to the President of the United States.
King	Name 10 things that you like to do.
Queen	Order your favorite meal.
Jack	Pretend two students don't know each other. Introduce them to each other.
Ten	Name five people you would like to meet and tell why for each.
Nine	Tell what you think is the best time of day and explain why.
Eight	Tell the most embarrassing incident that ever happened to you.
Seven	Describe the difference between an elephant and a cat.
Six	Give the steps involved in starting and driving a car.
Five	Tell how to find a book in the library.
Four	Name the three most important people in your life and explain why they are important.
Three	Describe the longest journey you have ever taken and tell why you took it.

Two	If you had the chance to do any one thing you wanted to do, what would it be and why.

♣ Clubs

Ace	Describe in detail your country's flag.
King	Name three holidays or festivals that are celebrated in your country of origin. Explain their significance and tell which is your favorite and why.
Queen	If you could take a trip to any place of your choice, all expenses paid, where would you go? Why? Who would you take with you?
Jack	If you could have an hour-long conversation with any person in the world, who would you choose? Why? (Assume you could speak each other's languages.)
Ten	If you could buy a gift for any person of your choice, what would you buy and who would you give it to? Why?
Nine	Which animal do you think makes the best pet? A bird, a dog, or a cat? What are your reasons?
Eight	Name three things you like about your country of origin and tell why you like them.
Seven	If you could be born again, would you like to be born again as the same sex or the opposite sex?
Six	Which would you rather be, left-handed or right-handed? Why?
Five	If you could become a world-class singer, what kind of a voice would you like to have, and what kind of music would you like to sing? Why?
Four	Which would you rather be, a symphony orchestra conductor, a lawyer, a doctor, or a movie actor? Explain your choice or supply one of your own.
Three	Suppose you could give a scholarship to a high school student so that student could attend a university of his or her choice. Who would you select, and why? (The student cannot be a member of your immediate family.)

Two   When you attend a university, is it better to live at home with your parents or is it better to live in a dormitory? Why?

Contributor   *Ted Plaister taught in the Department of ESL, University of Hawaii, for 24 years. He has also taught in Thailand, Japan, Micronesia, and American Samoa.*

◆ Using Audiovisual Aids Narrating With Video

Levels
Intermediate–advanced

Aims
Practice narrating and
describing events

Class Time
40–60 minutes

Preparation Time
20 minutes

Resources
Short videotape (20
minutes) of a single
story or part of a movie
List of the main events
of the story

The advantages of using videotapes in teaching listening have been recognized by many researchers in our field, including Underwood (1989) and Anderson and Lynch (1988). Yet, because it is difficult to find appropriate videos to match the students' levels, some teachers feel reluctant to use them. Underwood (1989) pointed out that what determines the difficulty of a text is not just the text itself but also what the students are asked to do with it. Thus, it is possible to have students focus on overall comprehension, rather than on trying to understand every word in the video.

Procedure

1. Find an appropriate video.
2. Prepare a list of events for each student.
3. Explain to the students that they will take turns watching the video and that those who see a specific part will have to describe it to those who do not.
4. Divide the class into Groups A and B.
5. Send Group A outside the classroom.
6. Start the video and let Group B watch it for about 5 minutes.
7. Ask Group A to come inside the classroom to pair up with a member of Group B.
8. After the 5 minutes, send Group B outside and let Group A watch the video.
9. Continue this procedure until the end of the video.
10. When the students have finished reporting to each other, give them the list of events and ask them to put the events in the right order. Have them work individually.
11. Check the students' answers and give feedback if necessary.

12. If time is available, have all the students watch the video together.

Caveats and Options

1. It is also possible to have the students work in groups and make predictions about the events in the story, instead of having them describe the events to each other.
2. The activity works best with small classes.

References and Further Reading

Anderson, A., & Lynch, A. (1988). *Listening.* Oxford: Oxford University Press.

Underwood, M. (1989). *Teaching listening.* London: Longman.

Contributor

Ada Angel Adaros is a graduate student in the TESOL program at Temple University Japan.

Recorded Chain Story

Levels
High beginning +

Aims
Practice out-of-class
speaking, listening, and
creative storytelling

Class Time
1 hour

Preparation Time
30 minutes

Resources
Audiotape
Access to audiotape
recorders outside of
class

Many students have difficulty when it comes to speaking in extended transactional turns. Brown and Yule (1983) note that explicit teaching of the spoken form should include work with extended transactional turns. One of the features of extended discourse is the use of temporal connectors. In this activity, students practice using temporal connectors. Because it is difficult to give homework in speaking or listening classes, especially in an EFL setting, this activity fulfills an important function while adding a sense of continuity to the semester.

Procedure

1. Ask students if they remember any favorite folk tales they were told as children.
2. Explain that folk tales are a type of storytelling in which the same story is told over and over again. Another type of storytelling involves creating original stories from the imagination.
3. Briefly present the different temporal connectors used in extended speaking, for example, *at first, after, then, after that, finally.* Put several on the board.
4. Tell the class a short story either from your imagination or using a "skeleton story" such as those that can be found in Morgan and Rinvolucri's (1983) *Once Upon a Time.*
5. Tell the story twice. During the first listening, the students' task is to notice which of the temporal markers you used when telling the story.
6. During the second listening, the students' task is to listen for the answers to some basic comprehension questions you have put up on the board.

7. After students discuss these questions in small groups, you can elicit the answers.

8. You may wish at this point to have a student briefly retell the story.

9. To prepare students for the task they are to do at home, create a chain story in class. Begin with a story starter, and go around the class having students continue the story until it reaches its conclusion.

10. Encourage the use of temporal connectors.

11. As time is limited in an in-class story chain, students' turns will be rather short. Encourage them to take much longer turns when they are recording their story chains at home.

12. Divide students into groups of five to eight. Give each group an audiotape with a story starter that you have recorded for them. Their task will be to create a story that continues from the story starter you have given them. (If you give every group the same story, it will be interesting to compare them later.)

13. If the class meets on a weekly basis, each week a different student in the group will be responsible for continuing the story. They can take the tape home and listen to the story as many times as necessary to get a sense of how the story has unfolded, and then using their imagination, create and record the next part of the story.

14. Encourage students to record their part of the story off the top of their heads or from brief notes rather than reading a written script. Also encourage the use of temporal markers and consistency in terms of point of view.

15. After the first student has recorded the second part, you may want to play it for the group and check to see if they are on the right track. Their goal should be the use of creative imagination in creating a story that has as much continuity as possible from start to finish (for ideas on how to increase continuity, see Caveats and Options).

16. When the groups have finished, play the stories for the class. If you have used the same story starter, the students will be surprised at how quite different stories can develop from the same beginning.

Caveats and Options

1. To add more support for students, in addition to a story starter, you can add a "story ender."

2. Instead of a story starter, you could either provide students with a "skeleton story" or let them create their own before beginning.
3. To encourage a more personalized and relevant context, you might have the students write a number of story starters from which they could choose the best one.
4. Student access to a tape recorder is essential for this exercise. If you think this might present a problem for any of your students, you may want to brainstorm possible solutions with them before you begin.

References and Further Reading

Brown, G., & Yule, G. (1983). *Teaching the spoken language: An approach based on the analysis of conversational English.* Cambridge: Cambridge University Press.

Morgan, J., & Rinvolucri, M. (1983). *Once upon a time: Using stories in the language classroom.* Cambridge: Cambridge University Press.

Contributor

Eric Bray previously taught elementary school in the United States and Mexico. Currently, he is Academic Director of the Kyoto YMCA English School in Japan.

New Wine in Old Bottles: Teaching Speaking Through Translation

Levels
Intermediate +

Aims
Learn colloquial English phrases by applying traditional translation exercises to an innovative video dubbing activity

Class Time
6 hours for class of 30

Preparation Time
1 hour

Resources
2–3 minute segment from TV show or cartoon
VCR and monitor
Audiotape recorder

In an EFL situation, especially in Japan, students are sometimes hesitant or uncomfortable speaking English to each other because they tend to rely on their L1 for communication. This activity combines a skill many students are familiar with (translation) while adding the twist of dubbing over a TV show with their own voices in English.

Procedure

1. Record the portion of the show on a videotape and on audiotapes (one for each group in the class).
2. Divide the class into groups based on the number of speakers in the recording.
3. Have the students watch the video segment, write down the speakers' names, and have them decide which roles they will take.
4. If no transcription is available, have each student listen to the audiotape and transcribe the L1.
5. Have the students translate the script into English. (This can be assigned as homework, and you can check the translations if necessary.)
6. Each student in the group should have a copy of the whole translated script and should memorize it (not just their part). This is one of the basic rules of acting—if you only memorize your own lines, you won't know when you're supposed to speak.
7. Audiotape each group of students as they perform the script while viewing the videotape with the sound off so the timing is right. (Coach the students for intonation or pronunciation at this point.) The groups should do two or three recordings so you can choose the best one.

8. After all the groups have made their recordings, dub each group's best recording over the videotape so the characters in the TV show or cartoon look like they are speaking English. (This can be done with the VCR connected to an audiotape machine with the appropriate cables.)

9. Show the completed videos in class. Students are usually impressed at how well their classmates can perform.

Contributor

Naomi K. Fujishima received her MA in TESOL at the Monterey Institute of International Studies. She is currently developing an Intensive English Program curriculum and teaching at Kwansei Gakuin University in Nishinomiya, Japan.

Tell Me What You See

Levels
Low intermediate +

Aims
Learn to communicate
meaning fluently

Class Time
45 minutes

Preparation Time
None

Resources
Audiotape recorder and
blank tape

Many learners of ESL lose fluency when they speak in the target language. When a concern for accuracy becomes excessive, it may inhibit a natural flow of language and impede understanding. The present activity, which is essentially a story-telling activity, focuses learners' attention on the events in a story and forces them to communicate what they see without thinking too much about accuracy.

Procedure

1. Divide the students into four groups and give each group 10 minutes to prepare a 3-minute story. The story should involve a series of actions that can be acted out easily (e.g., somebody being robbed and helped by two passersby).
2. After each group prepares its story, have the groups mime the events in their stories in front of the class.
3. While Group 1 is miming, have all the members of Group 2 take turns orally describing the events of the story.
4. Audiotape the oral descriptions.
5. After Group 1 finishes, have Group 2 mime their own story while Group 3 orally describes the events. (Again, audiotape the oral descriptions.)
6. After every group has finished miming their own story and describing the story acted out by another group, play the audiotaped descriptions to the whole class.
7. Have the miming group comment on the interpretations of their story and have the whole class discuss the language used to communicate meaning.

Caveats and Options

1. This activity is best used to follow up a presentation of action verbs.
2. Follow these procedures for more advanced students:

   - Select and videotape a 10-minute TV news report showing four series of events.
   - Divide the class into four groups and play the news reports to the class (muting the commentary portion).
   - Have the members of each group take turns giving running commentaries on one series of events from the news show during the muted portion of the program.
   - Audiotape the students' commentaries and let students discuss their language after listening to the tapes. You may want to play the news report once more with the professional commentaries played aloud so that students may make comparisons.

3. Some students may need help with the vocabulary for this exercise. You may want to run through the news portion of the videotape and pinpoint problem words and phrases with students before recording their comments. (Be careful not to have too much discussion about the content of the reports so that students are motivated to make their own commentaries.)

Contributor

Judy Ho has taught ESL in Hong Kong and Australia. She is currently teaching in the Department of English, City Polytechnic of Hong Kong.

Secret Audio Pals

Levels
Intermediate +

Aims
Talk naturally for a
genuine reason

Class Time
10 minutes

Preparation Time
5 minutes

Resources
Audiotapes
(one/pair of students)

When students have to communicate for a genuine reason, not only do they use language in a natural way but they also are more motivated to speak. This activity is designed to be homework.

Procedure

1. Divide the class in half and pair off the students. However, do not let students know who their partner is.
2. Give half the students a tape with a number written on it and give the other half numbers corresponding to those on the tapes. (Have all the students write their name and number on a small piece of paper and give it to you to write down.)
3. Have the students audiotape themselves speaking as homework. (The first assignment should be to talk a little about themselves, but they should not say their names.)
4. Have the students who made the recordings bring their tapes to a subsequent class meeting to distribute to their partners.
5. Have the partners listen to the tape and record something new for their partners.
6. Students continue in this fashion, recording several minutes of conversation on any topic of choice.
7. Once the assignment is finished (several class periods, as determined by the teacher), students can try to guess who their partners are.

Caveats and Options

1. Pair off your students with students from another class in the school (e.g., another ESOL class or a class of native English speakers). Follow the same procedures by coordinating the recording assignments with the teacher from the other class, passing the tapes back and forth for

a set period of time. The classes can meet for a party at the end of the assignment to guess the identities of partners.

2. Use a videotape instead of an audiotape for interaction between two different classes. Instead of pairing students from the different classes, have each class make a video (on a subject of their choice) and exchange it with the other class.

Contributor

Jenifer Lucas-Uygun is an ESL instructor and doctoral student in Language Education at Rutgers University, New Jersey, in the United States. She received her BA in English and Foreign Languages and her MA in TESOL from West Virginia University.

Cloze Music Video

Levels
Intermediate +

Aims
Enjoy a creative,
interesting, and
stimulating listening
experience

Class Time
45–60 minutes

Preparation Time
30–40 minutes

Resources
Music video
VCR and monitor

Cloze exercises help students focus their listening. Using music videos is a way for students to concentrate on a certain listening task and for you to bring authentic communication into the classroom. For students interested in contemporary North American society, the social issues and dilemmas that are often the topic of music videos are interesting avenues for conversation. Music videos can be a means of introducing topics that may otherwise be difficult to introduce in classroom in more traditional ways. This activity is designed to appeal to visually oriented and aurally oriented students alike.

Procedure

1. Create a cloze exercise by listening to the music video and writing down the words, leaving out the words appropriate to the level of students in your class. (A random deletion method also works well.)
2. Hand out the cloze exercise to the students and encourage students to first fill in some of the blanks without hearing or seeing the song. Ask the students (in pairs) to guess at the meaning of the song as well as the title and solicit information they may already have concerning the artists.
3. Play the video until the fifth blank has been passed and put the video on pause while students fill in the blanks. (Time varies with student level.)
4. Repeat Step 3 for each section of the video until the end, and then play the video in its entirety as many times as desired.
5. Students work individually at first and compare their answers after the song has been completed. Do not give the correct answers until students have had an opportunity to talk and discuss the possible answers together.

6. Go over the answers with the class as a whole and replay the video once more so students can more accurately see and hear the answers.
7. As a whole-class activity, review vocabulary and idiom usag･ within the song.

Caveats and Options

Focus discussions (as a class or in pairs) on sequences in the video of interest to students. Explain and discuss reduced speech and formal/informal registers, questions about the artists' choice of wording, biographical information on the artists, and possible messages of the song. Students may also be interested in discussing whether the theme of the song differs from the story of the video.

Contributor

Michelle McGrath received an MA in TESOL from Biola University. She is currently an EFL instructor at Senzoku Gakuen College in Tokyo, Japan. She has taught at several institutions in California and has presented at various CATESOL conferences.

Self-Correction in Oral Production

Levels
High beginning +

Aims
Produce accurate and fluent speech

Class Time
15–30 minutes

Preparation Time
None

Resources
Audiotape recorder and tapes
Pictures

This activity, which employs student-generated language, encourages students to assess and correct their own mistakes and to make them aware of accurate oral production. It is best implemented in a language lab or at home where students have access to a tape recorder and can work individually. By correcting the mistake themselves, the students are better able to focus on specific language items that are problematic, so the tendency to repeat mistakes becomes less frequent. Also, the fact that the student can see the difference improves learning and increases motivation and greater progress.

Procedure

1. Have the student choose a picture or series of pictures and describe the picture into a tape recorder.
2. Have the student transcribe the description and turn it in.
3. Read the student's transcription onto a tape, but read it correctly, ignoring any mistakes the student may have made.
4. Have the students listen to your readings and correct their own transcription independently.

Caveats and Options

1. Have the students describe the same pictures and transcribe their speech once again.

2. Circle the students' mistakes in the transcription and have the students compare this version with the first transcription.

Contributor

Anna Mussman taught EFL in Israel for many years. She returned to the United States to study for her MA, with a concentration in TESOL, at the School for International Training (SIT). At present, she is Associate Peace Corps Director responsible for the TEFL program in Turkmenistan.

Video Analysis

Levels
Any

Aims
Establish criteria for
language development,
experience self-
observation, and reflect
on discourse
Focus on which
communicative skills
and strategies to
develop

Class Time
10 minutes/student
(taping and viewing)

Preparation Time
Variable

Resources
Video camera, tape, and
TV monitor
Flip chart and markers

Video Analysis involves students in performing different tasks. They focus on presentations and dialogues, observing themselves, and reflecting on their communication skills and learning process through class discussion and dialogue journal writing. This self-observation technique allows students to take on the dual role of both the observer and the observed. Video analysis enhances student involvement with error correction, documents progress, and increases awareness of identity in the target language. Self-observation has a positive impact on students' decision making, and promotes student initiative, self-confidence, growth, and change. Increased self-awareness enhances communication skills, self-assessment, self-expression, critical thinking, and cross-cultural understanding.

Procedure

1. Topics for the videotaping sessions can be varied. Have students share information about themselves, their cultures, their fieldtrips, U.S. culture and cross-cultural issues, student generated topics—just about anything that is relevant.
2. Talk to your students briefly about their expectations and objectives before taping them.
3. As the students write down their grammar mistakes, impressions, and comments while viewing the tape, do the same on a flip chart.
4. Have students correct themselves and then have their peers offer suggestions and feedback.
5. Clarify any doubts.
6. Create a written error-correction exercise based on your notes for the next class.
7. Assign journal writing for the following day—entries can be guided. Sample questions for the students' journals include:

- What was positive about your presentation?
- Did anything surprise you?
- What can be improved?
- What about your communication skills—is there anything you would like to change? What? Why?
- What did you learn about language through self-observation?
- What did you learn about yourself?

Caveats and Options

1. Audiotape students initially so as to prepare them for the video task that lies ahead. Always leave this audio-only option open for students, in case they feel overwhelmed by the video.
2. Also, depending on how many contact hours you have weekly, video sessions can be held once a week.
3. Remember to videotape the students performing the initial task again at the end of the course so that all of you can compare and contrast the footage and assess progress. The changes are sometimes very subtle, but they often are quite dramatic.
4. Videotape yourself before doing this activity in class. You will see how you respond to self-observation and be able to check the skills, strategies, and stress involved.

Contributor

Carla Reichmann, USIA English Teaching Fellow in Amazonia, Brazil, has more than 6 years of teaching experience in Brazil and the United States.

Pair Taping

Levels
Intermediate +

Aims
Develop fluency in
foreign language
classrooms

Class Time
None

Preparation Time
None

Resources
Audiotape recorders
and tapes

Learning to speak would seem to require more self-initiating participation than other language skills, so it makes sense to give students some say in how they do it. Those who decide to study on their own will be able to practice more frequently because they can set the times.

Procedure

1. Have students choose a partner and tape a 25- to 30-minute conversation for fluency practice. (Students can speak about anything they choose and can change partners weekly or more often.)
2. Have each pair of students put their finished tapes (marked with names and date) into a box for their use, so you can check and return them in that box or another the following week.
3. Listen momentarily to a few places on the tapes and give the students feedback by attaching very brief notes to the tape cases about such features as the nonnativelike nature of their speech, lengthy silences, use of the L1 .... Even this amount of checking will serve to remind everyone that they are being monitored.

Caveats and Options

1. Pair taping is a way to get intermediate-level foreign language students to work on fluency, even if their class is large or infrequent. My Japanese college students in their second year of a conversation course chose to do pair taping 4 days a week instead of attending their once-a-week 90-minute class. They showed significantly more improvement in fluency over the year than their classmates.
2. Research has suggested that students learning in such a way won't misinform or develop a pidgin, but will correct each other, be motivated by being in charge of their own study, be relaxed, and find speaking English easier and more enjoyable than before.

References and Further Reading

Schneider, P. (1993). Developing fluency with pair taping. *JALT Journal*, *15*.

Contributor

Peter Schneider teaches at Shiga University of Medical Science in Japan and is the author of books for English language education.

Budding Translators

Levels
High intermediate +;
homogeneous L1

Aims
Become familiar with
some features of native
speaker conversation
Learn that the same
message can be
expressed in different
ways to suit the context

Class Time
2 hours

Preparation Time
Variable

Resources
Audiotapes

High intermediate ESOL students often possess a good repertoire of linguistic and vocabulary items. Well-planned and stimulating activities trigger these students' interest in using their language actively. One way to achieve this is to use video because it arouses interest and provides stimulus to the learners. An added advantage of using video is that students can be exposed to the language used as well as to the paralinguistic features present in authentic communication. In order to learn to converse effectively, students are given an opportunity to analyze their performance in comparison with native speakers' performance.

Procedure

1. Record a 5- to 10-minute TV program or film extract of several people conversing. The extract should be accompanied by subtitles in the students' L1. Interviews of celebrities or episodes from movies are popular with students while shorter easier items such as children's programs and cartoons can be chosen to suit the level and interest of your students.
2. Introduce the activity, set the purpose, and explain the task to students.
3. Play the video extract once with the sound turned off.
4. Ask students to build up a mental picture of the situation involved, the roles and relationship of characters. Give some guiding questions (e.g., *Who do you think these people are? Where are they? What is the situation? What's their relationship?*).
5. Divide students into groups. Play the video again and ask groups to reconstruct the lines in English according to the information provided by the subtitles.
6. Pause at suitable intervals so that students can prepare the dialogues.

7. Allow up to 45 minutes for students to write, discuss, and practice their scripts, and provide assistance and feedback while students are on the task.
8. Ask groups to record their own version so that they can listen to it later for comparison.
9. Play the video extract together with the recording of each group. Try to get the class to listen critically to each version and to focus on the differences in language use.
10. Play the video extract with the original sound track on.
11. Have class discuss the differences students have observed between their own version and the original. The teacher and/or students can select focal points for discussion (e.g., choice of words, register and degree of formality, stress and intonation, gestures and body language).

Caveats and Options

1. Ideally, each group should make a recording that can be played to the rest of the class. If tape recorders are not available, the groups can perform the conversation when the teacher is playing the silent video extract again.
2. If the video segments are not accompanied by subtitles, modify the task to a guessing game in which students are asked to make sensible guesses of what the speakers said. Students are encouraged to be creative in this activity and you should accept any sensible guesses.
3. The interesting and creative nature of this activity increases students' participation in the task and motivates them to see how the target language is used by native speakers. In the role-play activity, the groups become a team of actors and actresses who are trying to immerse themselves totally in their roles.
4. A practical constraint of the activity is that it may be difficult to find suitable materials accompanied by good quality subtitles in students' L1. Also, some students may need warm-up activities to help them tune in.

Contributor

Pauline Tam is Assistant Lecturer at the City Polytechnic of Hong Kong, where she teaches reading, writing, and business communications. She has also taught EFL for many years in Hong Kong secondary schools.

Part II: Accuracy

◆ Functions

Interrupting and Asking a Question

Levels
Any

Aims
Practice interrupting to ask a question

Class Time
20–30 minutes

Preparation Time
30 minutes

Resources
Interrupting and Question Openers Handout (See Appendix below)

Many international students, particularly those from Asian countries, have a reputation for being quiet, even taciturn, in class. It may simply be that, in part, they lack the language gambits that they need to take their turn in class, or in conversation. This exercise is designed to give them some of the tools that they will need to interrupt, take their turn, and ask a simple question.

Procedure

1. Explain the interrupting openers. Make sure that the students understand that there are polite ways of breaking into a talk or conversation to ask a question or make a statement. Show the students how these gambits work, and have them practice saying them.
2. Clarify the question openers (in this case, in the past tense). Make sure that the students realize that this is a limited set of simple openers that can be used to ask a variety of questions about events in the past.
3. Provide some examples of how these openers can be expanded. ·
4. Explain that the interrupting openers can be combined with the question openers to form a complete turn. In other words, point out that you normally interrupt for a reason. In this case, the interrupting is done to ask a question.
5. Tell the students that you are going to do an exercise in which you will tell them about your life. They will have to interrupt you in order to ask you a question. Point out that each student must interrupt once before any student can interrupt a second time. (This should keep the more vocal students from dominating.)

141

6. Begin telling the story of your life. (I usually begin with the following: "When I was born, I was very, very young.") I tell them where I was born, how my family moved around the United States, where I went to school, and other relevant bits of biodata.
7. Often the students become interested in the story. (Yes, they are interested in their teacher as a person.) However, if you find yourself talking for more than a minute, it will be necessary to remind the students that it is their job to interrupt you. You may have to encourage the interrupting at first. After they begin interrupting, they will usually continue. However, they may need reminding from time to time.

Caveats and Options

1. Small groups can be formed with each of the members talking about their own lives and other members interrupting with questions.
2. This activity seems to work well at the beginning of the course. It not only introduces the students to the tools that they need to interrupt with a question, but also helps them to get to know the teacher and establishes an atmosphere of interactive discussion.

References and Further Reading

Keller, E., & Warner, S. T. (1979). *Gambits: Openers: The first of three modules*. Hull, Canada: Canadian Government Printing Office.

Appendix A: Sample Interrupting and Question Openers Handout

Interrupting Openers	Question Openers (in past tense)
Excuse me.	When did you ... ?
Sorry.	Where did you ... ?
Pardon me.	Why did you ... ?
May I cut in for a minute?	What did you ... ?
Could I interrupt a moment?	How did you ... ?
(from Keller & Warner, 1979)	

Contributor

J. D. Brown is on the graduate faculty of the Department of ESL at the University of Hawaii. He is interested in language testing, curriculum development, and research design.

Agreeing and Disagreeing

Levels
Intermediate

Aims
Practice giving and
responding to opinions

Class Time
30 minutes

Preparation Time
5 minutes

Resources
Whiteboard and marker
Ball (optional)

A lively and relaxed classroom atmosphere helps students learn a language. This activity encourages the students to exchange opinions in a nonthreatening situation. The activity also centers around topics that are familiar and of interest to the students. Students are free to express their views, and they are also required to clarify or support their opinions. Genuine communication as well as learning can thus take place in a relaxed classroom setting.

Procedure

1. Explain the task to the students. The students will be paired up and they will take turns giving opinions about each other and responding to each others' opinions.
2. Write on the board the different expressions students can use in expressing and responding to an opinion. The list may include *I think, I feel, as I see it,* in expressing an opinion; and *that's right, correct, exactly,* in agreeing; and *I'm afraid not, not really, not quite* in disagreeing.
3. Pair off the students randomly. Explain the task. Students should take turns giving an opinion about the partner's beliefs, likes, dislikes, hobbies, interests, abilities and skills. Their partner should then respond, by either agreeing or disagreeing. Each student should give at least three opinions. The response has to be given immediately after each opinion.
4. Encourage the students to use a different expression each time. Examples might include:

   - Opinion: I think you like eating fast food a lot as I have seen you at least twice at McDonald's.

- Response: Well, you're quite right. I especially like the french fries there.
- Opinion: I guess you enjoy listening to pop music.
- Response: Actually, I don't. I prefer classical music to pop music.
- Opinion: In my opinion, you are very shy since I seldom hear you speak in class.
- Response: Mm, in fact I don't think I'm shy. I seldom speak in class since I think it is not very polite.

Caveats and Options

1. After the pair work, the students can then give opinions in front of the whole class. This can be carried out as a class game.
2. In the game, the teacher throws a ball to a student. The one who catches it will be the starter. He or she will then throw the ball to someone in the class. The student who catches the ball will have to respond to the opinion given by the starter. After the first round, this responder then throws the ball to another student and the one who catches it has to respond to the opinion given by the previous responder. And so on.
3. The format in carrying out the class game can be modified depending on resources available. For example, it can be replaced by drawing lots, following the class number sequence, or by the random choice of the students themselves. If there is not enough time, this part can even be skipped.
4. Remind the students to avoid giving embarrassing and offensive comments, such as *I think you are stupid and lazy.*

Contributor

Teresa Loh teaches in the Department of English in the City Polytechnic of Hong Kong. She holds a BA in English Studies and an MA in Applied Linguistics.

Greet Me

Levels
Any

Aims
Practice introductions
Practice register
differences
Increase cultural
sensitivity

Class Time
30 minutes

Preparation Time
10 minutes

Resources
Small pieces of note
paper and fasteners

Greet Me is an enjoyable guessing game that allows students to interact with each other using different registers. Students have the opportunity to play with and develop a store of language of various registers. The constant mingling and interaction make it useful as a warm-up or icebreaking activity.

Procedure

1. Prepare in advance notes with different instructions on them. For example:

   - greet me—your friend
   - greet me—your boss
   - greet me—your classmate
   - greet me—your teacher

2. Discuss with students the register differences involved in face-to-face English interaction.
3. Fasten notes to students' shoulders and instruct them not to look at the one on their own shoulders.
4. Have students interact with each other, greeting each other according to what is instructed on the note of the person facing them.
5. After about 5 minutes, stop the activity and have the students guess what their note says.

Caveats and Options

1. This activity can be modified to teach people about social responsibility in treating minorities. In this instance, the note can contain a variety of positive and negative messages. For example:

Positive

- be happy to see me
- greet me
- be attracted to me
- be proud of me
- encourage me

Negative

- be disgusted by me
- be angry with me
- be ashamed of me
- ignore me

2. Students who do not want to participate are the observers. The students mingle. After a few minutes, those with negative messages retreat to the outer edges of the circle and sit down—they move out and down. Those with positive messages stay very happily in the center of the circle.

3. Ask the observers what they saw and then lead a discussion on how the students felt and what happens when someone has a negative label.

4. As a final activity, interact warmly with those who had negative labels and do a follow up activity on what the students can do to support minorities.

5. This activity should only be done with very mature students. It's a powerful teaching tool but also a very emotional one.

Contributor

Elizabeth Macdonald was a Peace Corps Volunteer in the Central African Republic and has trained EFL teachers for the Peace Corps. She received her MA in TESOL at the Monterey Institute of International Studies, where she is Director of the Intensive ESL Program.

Making Your Point

Levels
Intermediate +

Aims
Defend a particular
position, give
counterarguments and
rebuttals

Class Time
Several class periods

Preparation Time
20 minutes

Resources
None

This activity helps students improve critical thinking skills by letting them argue both for and against a particular point of view or position. Students must think not only of supporting statements for their position, but also opposing statements and why they are inadequate or inferior to their original argument or position.

Procedure

1. Explain the steps of a persuasive argument and present the following format for the activity:

   - Introduction and statement of position
   - Reasons for position
   - Counterarguments to position
   - Rejection (rebuttal) of counterarguments
   - Summary statement and conclusion.

2. Take a position that can be worked through fairly easily with the class (e.g., to reduce air pollution, all cars should be banned in major cities of the world by the year 2000) and have students help you come up with the pros and cons of the position. Model the activity for students by rejecting the opposing arguments and restating why the original position is the best one.

3. You may have students come up with several other sample topics until they feel comfortable with the five stages of argumentation and understand the importance of coming up with con arguments they might not agree with personally.

4. Review some of the rhetorical markers used in arguing positions (e.g., *I believe that..., It is my opinion that..., Let me repeat that..., The reason(s) I take this position..., The reason(s) I reject that*

argument..., I hope you can see/understand that..., The problem with that argument is...).

5. Have students choose an issue or position they would like to argue (the class can brainstorm a list) and ask them to prepare for class discussion using the argumentation format explained above.
6. Conduct this argumentation format in class discussions until student have each had a chance to argue their positions.

Caveats and Options

Divide students into teams and give them opposing sides of a position. Give students several minutes to discuss their positions and have each team go through the argumentation format. The teacher or another student may serve as moderator, calling time as necessary. The rest of the class decides which team's argument is more convincing.

Contributor

Craig Machado teaches in an academic ESL program at Oregon State University in the United States. He has taught community college and was in the Peace Corps in West Africa in the 1970s.

The Yes/No Game

Levels
Beginning–intermediate

Aims
Increase fluency with
question forms

Class Time
10 minutes

Preparation Time
None

Resources
Gong, tin lid, and
spoon, or whistle
List of questions
appropriate to students'
level

The Yes/No Game gives students intensive practice in using interrogative forms in spoken English. The intensity of this practice is made possible by the gamelike nature of the activity and its structure. The game should complement classroom studies on asking for personal information.

Procedure

1. Familiarize students with a variety of question types and forms (e.g., *Have you got any . . . ?, Do you live in/with . . . ?, Do you like . . . ?, How long have you been studying . . . ?, Were you born in . . . ?*).
2. Demonstrate the Yes/No Game with one of the more extroverted students in front of the class, explaining that the object of the game is to answer questions without using yes or no. Model several questions.
3. Call on students to be the questioners and have them ask several questions in quick succession.
4. Each student must answer the question in 5 seconds and is not allowed to answer by shaking or nodding of the head or making assenting or dissenting noises. (Have students respond using forms such as *That's correct, I am not . . . , It is true to say that . . .*).
5. Have each student try and answer questions for 1 minute without saying either yes or no.
6. Sound the gong once if a student uses yes or no and move onto the next student. If a student answers questions successfully for 1 minute, sound the gong twice and declare a winner.

Caveats and Options

Divide the class into groups of three and have one person in the group be the questioner, one be the responder, and the third be the yes/no monitor and time keeper (clapping their hands instead of using a gong).

Contributor

Dino Mahoney is Senior Lecturer in the English Department at the City Polytechnic of Hong Kong.

The Selling Game

The Selling Game provides a creative, gamelike setting in which students can explore the language of persuasion and negotiation in a series of motivating, open-ended, ongoing oral interactions.

Procedure

1. Gather a bag of unlikely products that students will have to try and sell to each other. (The objects in the bag should be things that don't have immediate purchase appeal and are difficult to sell.)
2. Divide the class in half between sellers and buyers.
3. Have all the sellers come to the front of the class pull one of the objects from the bag.

4. Have the buyers and sellers mingle, with the sellers trying to interest buyers into purchasing their product. The sellers must think of as many uses as possible for the product, and buyers may haggle over the price set by the seller if they think it's too high. Buyers must make a purchase by the end of the game.

5. After the sale, have the seller make a note of any money that would be exchanged and move on to the next buyer. (The seller retains the product as a sample to show to the next buyer.)
6. Close the market after 10–15 minutes and have the sellers add up the value of their sales. The student who has made the most money is the winner.
7. Return the objects to the bag and repeat the activity with students changing roles.

Caveats and Options

1. Do the activity as a telephone sales game if it is difficult to set up a free mixing situation in the classroom. No objects are required.

   - Have students sit in pairs back to back, with one student acting as the sales person and the other as the customer.
   - Announce an item to be sold, and have students engage in telephone sales negotiation.
   - Have the customers report with a show of hands if they were persuaded to buy the product.
   - Reverse the roles and introduce a new item for sale.

2. It may be beneficial to explain and model words and phrases that are typical of sales situations, either in person or on the telephone. Develop a worksheet of common language used in sales situations appropriate to the level of your students.
3. The success of the game depends on the buyers not being too intransigent. Get across the concept that purchasing an item is a reward for the persuasive oral skills of the seller and should not necessarily be based on the desirability of the item (i.e., the higher the price of the purchase, the higher the buyer has rated the seller's persuasive oral skills).

Contributor

Dino Mahoney is Senior Lecturer in the English Department at the City Polytechnic of Hong Kong.

My Advice Is . . .

Levels
Intermediate

Aims
Focus on seeking and
giving advice and
expressing opinions

Class Time
30–40 minutes

Preparation Time
1 hour

Resources
Photocopied, advice-
seeking letters and
replies from magazines
or newspapers

This activity creates a setting in which students explore, in a guided but self-determining fashion, the expression and modification of opinion. Students will also be able to practice ways in which advice can be solicited and given. The activity sensitizes students to how different settings influence spoken interaction (e.g., how giving advice to someone not in front of you and giving advice face-to-face differ).

Procedure

1. Find and photocopy advice-seeking letters with published responses that are appropriate and stimulating for the age, cultural background, and group personality of your class.
2. Arrange students into groups of four.
3. Raise interest in the issues that will be addressed later in the advice-seeking letters by asking a few relevant questions (e.g., if the letter is about an intolerable amount of homework given to students, you may ask if students think they get too much homework).
4. Give each group copies of the same advice-seeking letter. (Do not give them the published replies yet.)
5. Have the students in each group read the letter, and discuss the vocabulary and main ideas. (You should monitor the discussions and help answer questions where necessary.)
6. Have each group formulate the advice they would give the writer. (One member of the group should be taking notes.)
7. After these discussions, invite feedback and discussion by the class as a whole.
8. Distribute copies of the published reply letter and ask students to discuss them in their groups. (You may bring these discussions back to the whole class also.)

9. Have students simulate a face-to-face discussion with the letter writers as a way to further explore the issues raised and verbally practice giving opinions and advice. (The interviewing student can play the role of a friend, relative, or teacher. Encourage all players at this stage to improvise any necessary but unstated background information.)

Caveats and Options

1. Follow the activity with a class debate if the issues raised are broad enough and the whole class shows sufficient interest.
2. As a written follow-up assignment, have each student write an advice-seeking letter. Distribute the letters to the class for individual written answers.

Contributor

Dino Mahoney is Senior Lecturer in the English Department at the City Polytechnic of Hong Kong.

Letting Students Ask the Questions

Levels
Any

Aims
Speak and learn about
an interesting topic
Take responsibility for
learning

Class Time
15–30 minutes

Preparation Time
20 minutes

We all know that people want to talk about what interests them. This activity makes the most of that premise by requiring students' participation throughout every step: from allowing the students to choose the topics to be discussed to having the students be responsible for leading the group discussions.

Procedure

1. Give students a questionnaire asking them to list at least five topics they would like to discuss.
2. Type the list of topics on a handout for students and have them choose (as a class) a topic to discuss in the next lesson.
3. Have students write down three interesting and relevant questions about the topic they would like to ask other students.
4. For the next lesson:

   - Type the questions and number them on a handout.
   - Cut out as many slips of paper as there are questions and number them corresponding to the questions on the handout.
   - Include vocabulary items on the handout that may be useful for the upcoming discussion.

5. On the discussion day, give the students the handout and distribute the slips of paper at random so that each student has a few slips.
6. Have students ask the question that corresponds to the number on their slip of paper, beginning with Question 1. Each student asking a question should actively elicit responses from the other students and make sure everyone has a chance to speak.

7. Continue the same process until all the questions have been asked and discussed.

Caveats and Options

During the first few lessons, it is helpful to teach students some discourse skill and phrases for discussions (e.g., *Well, you have a point there, but I feel that...* instead of *You're wrong!*). Teach the students how to give their opinions, ask others for their opinions, agree, disagree, and hedge. Once they have learned the art of discussing a topic diplomatically, feelings can be spared and students will be more willing to express their thoughts.

Contributor

Tracy M. Mannon teaches at the University of Neuchâtel in Switzerland. She has also taught in Beijing, China, and at the University of Delaware.

The Year That Was

Levels
Any

Aims
Discuss important
events that occurred in
the previous year
Practice arguing,
agreeing, disagreeing,
and justifying

Class Time
2 hours

Preparation Time
30 minutes

Resources
Copy of *Time,
Newsweek, Life,* or any
other magazine that
summarizes the past
years' events in photos
Chalkboard and chalk

Nearly everyone has access to media news and may discuss the news in their L1. As language teachers, we can capitalize on this real-life activity outside the classroom and encourage students to express their opinions about the news in a classroom activity.

Procedure

1. Choose, cut out, and paste onto separate sheets of paper, 10 pictures about news stories from a previous year out of an end-of-the-year magazine. (Do not leave any captions or text on the pictures.)
2. Number the pictures from 1 to 10 in random order (i.e., no particular order of importance or time). You may need to make several sets of pictures, depending on the size of the class.
3. Have students use a clean sheet of paper and write Topic at the top of the left-hand side, and Comment at the top of the right-hand side. Also have them number from 1 to 10, at equal intervals, down the left-hand side of the page.
4. Tell students you will distribute 10 pictures. They should look at them and write the topic of the story (if they know it) next to the corresponding number on the Topic side of their page (e.g., Earthquake in Japan). Students should not discuss the pictures with you or other classmates during this part of the activity.
5. Organize the class into groups of five and have students compare their topic lists. (Give each group access to the complete set of pictures so they may check their topics.)
6. Once you and the students are satisfied with the lists, elicit the topics from students as a class activity and write them on the chalkboard so that eventually, everyone has a similar list.

7. Have the groups discuss the topics for 15–20 minutes, and have them make notes under the Comment section of their paper (e.g., Osaka, Japan endured a severe earthquake last year, but nobody was killed).
8. Choose members from each group to explain to the class what the 10 news items are about.
9. Make brief notes from this discussion on the board.
10. Ask groups to discuss the importance of each item and rank them in order of importance. (Try and select pictures of fairly equal importance when preparing this lesson.)
11. Again, choose members from each group to tell the class the order of importance they have determined, and encourage class discussion to decide the "best" order.

Caveats and Options

1. As a follow-up activity, have the same groups create lists based on categories of news items (e.g., sports, movies, local events, funny stories, or stories they would have liked to see in the news).
2. This activity is most useful at the beginning of the new calendar year, especially if it is also the beginning of a new course, because it offers a lot of student talking time and gives everyone the chance to work cooperatively.

Contributor

Lindsay James Miller is a lecturer in the English Department at City Polytechnic of Hong Kong. He has taught English in Europe, the Middle East, and Southeast Asia for the past 13 years.

Using a Box of Raisins to Promote Speech

Levels
Low intermediate +

Aims
Generate speech that covers a broad range of linguistic skills plus some simple mathematics

Class Time
Variable

Preparation Time
Very little

Resources
One small box of raisins/student

This activity involves overall listening comprehension, some cultural understanding, and the development of some content-area knowledge. Students focus on understanding as much as they can about raisins as well as other information—not on language learning per se. There is also an element of fun in using this simple learning aid. The use of a teaching aid—something as common and ordinary as small boxes of raisins—demonstrates how just about anything can be used for productive language teaching and learning. Nowhere does it say ESL or EFL on a box of raisins, but this in no way lessens its value as an L2 teaching aid. Rather, appropriate use of a prop such as this proves clearly that the world can be one's English-teaching oyster.

Procedure

1. Pass out boxes of raisins, one to a student with the caution not to open the boxes. Ask the students to study the boxes for a minute or two.
2. Working with the class as a whole, ask individual students questions about what is on the box (e.g., *How many colors can you find on the box? Name them. Describe the girl on the front of the box. What is she holding in her hands? What does _____ mean?* [Here refer to the various abbreviations used on the box about weights, patent office registration, and the like.] *What is the girl wearing on her head?*) Continue this activity until all material on the outside of the box has been covered.
3. Ask the students to open their boxes, but tell them not to eat the raisins.

4. Provide the students with a clean piece of paper and have them remove the raisins and count them.

5. Then ask the students to report their number of raisins individually to a monitor who writes the numbers in a column on the chalkboard.

6. Have another student total the numbers and write the sum at the bottom.

7. Ask a third student to then calculate the average number of raisins per box and report this to the class.

8. Ask the students individually how many raisins they had in their boxes. Teach the answer by writing on the chalkboard: *I had X raisins in my box. This was above average/average/below average.*

9. Once students have the reply memorized, erase the answer and query each student so they answer in a more conversational style.

10. Continue a question and answer session with the students using questions on the order of: *What were raisins before they became raisins? What is the process called?* (Teach *dehydration* or *sun drying.*) *What countries are the major raisin producers?* (This may require some encyclopedia work.) *How are raisins used besides being eaten "as is"? How would you describe a raisin to someone who hasn't seen one before?* (This is difficult.)

11. For the culminating activity, allow the students to eat their raisins. Ask them to describe the taste. (This is also difficult to do. The usual answer is "sweet." But does this really explain what a raisin tastes like?)

Caveats and Options

1. Rather than working with the class as a whole, put the students in small groups. Then, after suitable discussion, have them write down their findings about what they see on the box. They can then designate one student to report their findings to the class. You can act as a guide so as to ensure that each group has a chance to respond. The other class activities may then be replicated by the groups and the appropriate comparisons made.

2. For homework, assign the students to find out additional information on raisins in the library, most probably using the encyclopedia. Group work can be involved with one group reporting on the countries where raisins are grown commercially; another group can

report on cultural practices required to grow grapes, for example, the type of soil suitable for grape production; still another group can gather statistical data on raisin production for the past, say, 10 years, the value of this crop, and so forth.

3. Other possibilities include investigating supermarkets to see how many brands of raisins there are, the price, and so on; surveying the indices of cookbooks to discover the different ways raisins are used in recipes.

Contributor

Ted Plaister taught in the Department of ESL, University of Hawaii for 24 years. He has also taught in Thailand, Japan, Micronesia, and American Samoa.

Giving Simple Directions

Levels
High beginning +

Aims
Practice listening
comprehension

Class Time
Variable

Preparation Time
Minimal

Resources
Eight plastic glasses
Four different food
colorings
Water

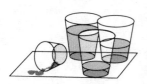

Caveats and Options

L earning to follow directions is a very important skill for any learner and doing so in an L2 is crucial. This exercise provides practice in an interesting, gamelike environment.

Procedure

1. Fill four of the glasses with water and put a different color in each one so as to have four colors.
2. Put the four glasses in a random cluster on a desk at the front of the room.
3. Select a student and hand that student a card printed with:

   Arrange the glasses in a row from left to right as follows: First color is red, second is green, third is orange, and the fourth is purple.

4. Select a second student who is to follow the directions printed on the first student's card.
5. Have the first student then read what is on the card so that everyone can hear while the second student complies.
6. Have the members of the class monitor the activity closely. If there is an error, they should raise their hands and point this out.
7. Repeat with subsequent pairs of students.

1. Many different combinations may be taught. If possible, have the students generate the directions.
2. Some suggested directions for students follow:

   - Pour half of the red water into an empty glass.
   - Put the two red glasses on either side of the glass with the green water in it.

- Pour half of the green water into an empty glass. Now alternate (this word will probably have to be taught) the red and green glasses beginning with a red glass.

3. Use more glasses so as to involve more students. This will provide some competition between teams to see who can follow the directions without making any errors.
4. How involved to make an activity of this type is a function of class size, time available, and the linguistic proficiency of the students. For advanced students, the Simon Says element may be introduced when giving directions, especially if the students can handle the directions being given at a rapid pace. For this type of variation, the teacher should give the directions rather than having a student read them.
5. A type of Total Physical Response activity may be included to expand the exercise (e.g., pick up the red glass with your left hand; transfer it to your right hand; hand the glass to a student who is wearing something red . . .).

Contributor

Ted Plaister taught in the Department of ESL, University of Hawaii for 24 years. He has also taught in Thailand, Japan, Micronesia, and American Samoa.

◆ Grammar
Travel Talk Round Table

Levels
Intermediate +

Aims
Review present perfect
and time expressions
ever/never
Contrast present perfect
with simple past and
ago
Practice distinction
between /b/ and /v/

Class Time
30–70 minutes

Preparation Time
None

Resources
Chalkboard, chalk,
paper, and pencils

This small-group and whole-class activity stimulates students to inquire and speak about their classmates' and their own travel experiences. Travel Talk Round Table is a welcome way to escape a textbook, increase students' individual turns at talk, encourage students to learn about each other, contextualize grammar and pronunciation in genuine communication, and keep students' eyes up when they speak.

Procedure

1. Have the class brainstorm and call out names of any countries they can think of while the instructor or a student writes the country names on the chalkboard.
2. When there are 30 or more country names on the board, divide the class into pairs or small groups.
3. Write this model conversation on the chalkboard so that everyone can see it:
   Have you ever been to _____? — Yes, I have. / No, I haven't.
4. Choose country names from the chalkboard and model the conversation with a student.
5. After the student answers, write the country name and Yes or No on the chalkboard to show how to take notes.
6. Tell the class to write down countries with both Yes and No answers when they interview another student.
7. In their pairs or groups, have students take turns interviewing each other using the model question, country names, and model short answers from the chalkboard.
8. During this time, circulate among the groups to check that each student has at least two or three Yes answers to help with pronunciation of /b/ and /v/ and to facilitate students' note-taking.

9. After students have asked their interviewees about 10–15 countries, stop the interviews and put the class in a round table setting so that all students can see each other.

10. Write this model sentence on the chalkboard:
[Student] has been to _____ , but s/he has never been to _____ .

11. Model the sentence several times using different students' names and country names.

12. Now turn the talk over to students in the round table.

13. Have a volunteer begin with the model sentence to tell the class about the student he or she interviewed. (The volunteer should use one Yes and one No country from his/her interview notes.)

14. Go around the room with students repeating until everyone has used all information from the interviews.

15. When speakers have only Yes or only No countries left, have them make complex sentences with *and* for Yes countries and *or* for No countries (instead of *but*).

Caveats and Options

1. Advanced students' model questions/answers for interviews are:
Have you ever been to _____? → No, I haven't.
Have you ever been to _____? → Yes, I have.
How long ago were you there? → I was there ____ years/months ago.

2. Advanced students' round table model sentences are:
[Student] has never been to_____ , but s/he has been to _____ . S/he was there _____ years/months ago.

3. Possible extensions of the activity are a listening memory game to determine who has traveled the most or a review of the intonation of yes/no questions and short answers.

Contributor

Beverly J. Beisbier, Instructor at the University of California, Berkeley Extension, has developed ESOL courses and materials and taught in the United States and France.

Get It Done

Levels
Intermediate +

Aims
Practice causative *get*
or *have*
Review regular and
irregular past participles
and pronunciation of
-ed endings
Understand English
spoken at normal,
conversational speed

Class Time
20–25 minutes

Preparation Time
None

Resources
Chalkboard and chalk

This class activity encourages learners to gain confidence in control over one of the many uses of the verb *get*. Get It Done encourages students to avoid dependency on written English for oral work, contextualize grammar and pronunciation in genuine communication, and keep their eyes up when they speak.

Procedure

1. Put two or three examples of causative *get* or *have* sentences on the chalkboard. For example,

   - Joseph gets his hair cut every three weeks.
   - She got her teeth checked at the dentist.
   - New students will get their registration verified soon.

2. Elicit from the class the meaning of causative *get* by asking such questions as, *Does Joseph cut his own hair? Who probably cuts his hair?*
3. Have the class articulate a rule for using causative *get* (e.g., when the subject of the sentence arranges for an action to take place; the subject of the sentence is not doing the action).
4. After analyzing the examples, the class then explains how to form causative *get* (e.g., *get* + noun + past participle).
5. Change the examples on the chalkboard as follows:

   - Joseph gets it cut every three weeks.
   - She got them checked at the dentist.
   - New students will get it verified soon.

6. Have the class revise their explanation of causative *get* formation based on these new examples (e.g., get + noun/pronoun + past participle).

7. Write these model conversations on the chalkboard:

Conversation 1
  Speaker A: My battery is dead!
  Speaker B: You should *get* it *charged*.

Conversation 2
  Speaker A: My teeth hurt!
  Speaker B: You should *get* them *checked*.

8. Now tell the class you are going to complain, and they need to respond with advice using causative *get* as in the models. Use the following complaints or create your own. Call on students to respond or wait for volunteers. For example,

My coat is stained!	All of my shirts are wrinkled!
My hair looks terrible!	This essay needs proofreading!
The TV is broken!	My skirt is too short!
My car won't start!	The gas tank is empty!
This knife is blunt!	My shoes are too tight!
These pants are too long!	I can't translate this letter!
My eyes hurt!	My glasses are broken!
The roof leaks!	

9. If a student uses singular instead of plural pronouns or if *-ed* is not pronounced, you may prefer not to go on with the next complaint. Instead, repeat the complaint and point at the key word or ending on the chalkboard before the student responds a second time.

Caveats and Options

1. Intermediate students may need some sample verbs on the chalkboard to be able to respond appropriately to the complaints (e.g., *iron, shorten, lengthen, proofread, [hair] dye, [hair] dress, [shoes] stretch, sharpen*).

2. Advanced students may be introduced to and practice both causative *get* and *have*. Be sure to vary the examples on the chalkboard and encourage students to use both in their responses.
3. To increase each individual's practice time, have students complain to each other in pairs or small groups and respond with causative *get* or *have*.

References and Further Reading

Celce-Murcia, M., & Larsen-Freeman, D. (1983). *The grammar book: An ESL/EFL teacher's course*. Rowley, MA: Newbury House.

Contributor

Beverly J. Beisbier, Instructor at the University of California, Berkeley Extension, has developed ESOL courses and materials and taught in the United States and France.

Before and After

Levels
Advanced

Aims
Practice modal
auxiliaries *should* and
*must have + past
participle*
Review pronunciation
of *-ed* endings

Class Time
25 minutes

Preparation Time
2–3 hours (first time
only, materials may be
reused)

Resources
Magazines, newspapers,
flyers, junk mail, and
other advertisements
Stiff paper or index
cards
Glue or tape

This small-group activity provides a communicative context for using *should* to express advice and *must have + past participle* to express past probability and increase learners' vocabulary. Frequent repetition of regular past participles encourages contextualized practice for pronunciation of *-ed* endings.

Procedure

1. Prepare material to stimulate oral production, using ads with "before and after" pictures. (e.g., cosmetic make-overs, auto body repairs, auto body repainting, glasses to contact lenses, hair restoration, cosmetic surgery, weight loss, home remodeling [exterior, kitchen, bathroom, landscaping], upholstery/rug cleaning and repair, photo touch ups, body building, no-sun tanning products, hairdos ...).
2. Choose pairs in which the "before" pictures most clearly show that some action needs to be taken to correct the damage or problem.
3. Cut out the pictures and mount the "before" pictures on one set of cards and the "after" pictures on another set.
4. Write names on the cards for pictures of people; for pictures of homes, cars, yards, for example, write *Joan's kitchen* or *Nick's car*.
5. Begin the activity by distributing the "before" picture cards to small groups of students.
6. Ask the groups what each person on the cards should do to beautify herself, fix his car, remodel her home ....
7. Have students in each group then talk about each "before" picture card using the word *should*.
8. When students have finished creating their *should* sentences, distribute the "after" picture cards.

9. While members of each group compare the "before" and "after" pictures, ask the groups what each person must have done to beautify herself, fix his car, remodel her home . . . .

10. Students in each group then talk about the "after" picture cards using *must have + past participle*.

11. During the activity, circulate among the groups to check that each student is creating sentences correctly and is pronouncing *-ed* endings on regular past participles.

12. Elicit a variety of verbs from peers if students' vocabulary range is limited. Regular verbs for *-ed* might include:

trim	lighten	lift
remove	lengthen	restore
install	shorten	remodel
paint	repair	landscape
repaint	mount	curl
mow	replace	dye
change	move	tint
darken	reduce	increase

Caveats and Options

1. If *should* and *must have + past participle* are being taught or reviewed during separate class meetings, do the "before" picture cards during the *should* class meeting.

2. Distribute both the "before" and "after" picture cards during the *must have + past participle* class meeting.

3. Cover the picture cards with clear contact paper if you would like to use them again. This is especially important for newspaper pictures, which will yellow or become brittle.

4. Have students interview one another in pairs about something they have changed, fixed, or repaired. They can then report to the rest of the class what their partners did.

References and Further Reading

Celce-Murcia, M., & Larsen-Freeman, D. (1983). *The grammar book: An ESL/EFL teacher's course*. Rowley, MA: Newbury House.

Contributor

Beverly J. Beisbier, Instructor at the University of California, Berkeley Extension, has developed ESOL courses and materials and taught in the United States and France.

Total Physical Response Verb Practice

Levels
Beginning; children

Aims
Practice pronunciation, questions, and answers with familiar verbs

Class Time
15 minutes

Preparation Time
5–10 minutes

Resources
Pocket chart
Index cards

An old Chinese proverb states: "I hear and I forget, I see and I remember, I do and I understand." Performing actions enables young L2 learners to learn verbs and verb tenses quickly and easily. The game format makes it enjoyable. In addition, you can easily assess the students' knowledge.

Procedure

1. Seat the students in a circle. Perform an action and ask the students to say what you are doing (e.g., *You are walking*).
2. If the student's answer is correct, have the child perform a different action and ask, "What am I doing?" This student then calls on another for the answer.
3. Continue until all of the students have had a few turns.

Caveats and Options

1. Write physical actions on index cards.
2. Have a student pick a card with an action written on it and perform that action. The other students guess what their classmate is doing. The student who guesses correctly picks the next card and performs the action.
3. Separate students into groups of four with a high-achieving student, a low-achieving student, and two average-achieving students in each group. Give each group three cards describing an action (e.g., one card has *am,* one card has *I,* and one card has *jumping*). The three children hold up their cards and get in line in the correct word order and the fourth child performs the action.

4. Adapt the activity for higher levels by using more difficult verbs, by writing compound or complex sentences on the cards, and/or by including more reading tasks.

Contributor

Judi Braverman is a K–5 ESL teacher at Lindell Elementary School in Long Beach, New York in the United States. She has trained student teachers from Adelphi University and Hofstra University.

Why Questions

Levels
Beginning–intermediate

Aims
Form Why questions
quickly

Class Time
Several minutes

Preparation Time
Minimal

Resources
Chart or photocopies
Paper and pencil

This activity can be used easily and effectively in pairs to simulate language laboratory practice. It also encourages creativity if the learners make up their own examples and allows self-regulation, not to mention all the other advantages of pairwork.

Procedure

1. Pair off the students.
2. Give students a sheet with the answers given below.
3. Tell the students to ask Why questions for each statement given by their partners. For example,
   Dracula was sad. Why was he sad?
   Because he couldn't suck any blood.
   Because there were no humans around.
   Because he was in the Arctic.
   Because his plane crash-landed.
   Because it had engine trouble.
   Because it was old.
   Because the previous owner didn't replace it.
   Because he died.
   Because a female vampire bit him . . . .

Caveats and Options

1. Pairs of students can then prepare further examples on topics of personal interest to be exchanged with other pairs. The topics might range from the imaginary to true statements, such as *Labour lost the election again*.
2. If there is real enthusiasm, the class could build up a bank of such activities.

3. The activity works by itself and the format is simple but versatile. However, because the activity is controlled, it is also limited.
4. If the students make up other examples, the preparation time will vary.

Contributor

Anthony Bruton has trained teachers in Brazil, Singapore, and Spain. He now teaches methodology in Spain at the University of Seville. This activity is adapted from an idea in Julian Dakin's The Language Laboratory and Language Learning *(1973, Longman).*

Verb Pass for Fluency Development

Levels
Any

Aims
Freely use common and less common verbs

Class Time
Variable

Preparation Time
None

Resources
Paper and pencils, or chalkboard and chalk

This exercise allows students to focus on describing the details of every-day life while orally practicing the simple past tense of verbs. Students practice digging for words to express as many activities as possible.

Procedure

1. Have the class begin with a discussion of their activities over the past weekend, for example.
2. Have the students take turns using the following format:

   - Each student uses a minimum of five past tense verbs to describe the activities.
   - The sixth verb is passed to the next student as an incomplete sentence and that student must incorporate it into a description of his or her own activities.
   - One person keeps track of the verbs used (either on the board or on paper), and no verb can be repeated.

3. The exercise continues like this and the list of more common verbs gradually becomes exhausted until students are forced to search for and use less common verbs.
4. A typical conversation may proceed like this:

   A: Last weekend I *went* shopping, I *watched* TV and I *ate* lunch with a friend. We *saw* a movie and after that *drank* a soda at a restaurant. On Sunday, I *drove* . . .

   B: On Sunday, I *drove* with a friend to the mountains. We *hiked* for a few hours. We *enjoyed* the fresh air. I *slept* for a long time after that. Later, I *talked* to a friend on the phone. I *washed* . . .

175

C: *I washed* the dog and *worked* in the garden . . . .

5. Tell students that statements do not necessarily have to be true.

Caveats and Options

1. After using this exercise in English conversation courses with shy Japanese high school students, I found that students came to class prepared and expecting to speak. They clearly enjoyed the challenge, although the person who went first had an advantage.
2. Vary the number of verbs required by each person or assign a different tense.
3. Use another procedure to help low-level students:

   - Before beginning, have students think of as many verbs as possible and write them on the board. Sometimes these words will have to be changed to the past form.
   - As students take turns, have them refer to the board for an unused verb and check off used verbs.

Contributor

Diane Huntoon is a graduate of the University of California, Santa Barbara, and has been teaching English in Japan for 4 years.

Tell Me More About It

Levels
Intermediate +

Aims
Use linguistic
knowledge of WH-
questions to seek and
give information
Turn written
information into speech

Class Time
1 hour

Preparation Time
None

Resources
None

Because information seeking and giving are so important, this simulation exercise makes students aware of the relevance of such functions to their daily lives and hence the importance of improving their skills. By asking students to collect and obtain information brochures on different products, real-life situations or enquiries can be brought into the classroom.

Procedure

1. Ask students to obtain a brochure of a commercial product, a course, a real estate deal, or a package tour before class starts.
2. Have students work in pairs, with one simulating the role of a potential customer making the enquiry, and the other acting as a sales agent answering the enquiry and supplying information in the brochure on the product. After the enquiry simulation, ask the students to change roles so that each student will have a chance to make an enquiry as well as answer it.
3. Give students 5 minutes to find out from their partners the type of product they are supposed to make enquiries about. Ask the students to make a list of the requirements and qualities they look for in the product and to think of the information they would like to obtain from their simulation partners and make a list of Wh-questions they will be putting to them before making the enquiry.
4. At the end of the role simulation, ask students to report to the class as to how well the product fits into their requirements and whether they are going to buy it.

Caveats and Options

1. Have students work in pairs, with one trying to guess the product the other has researched without asking what it is exactly, and the other supplying information and answering any questions except

what the product is. When one partner comes up with a good sense of the product, the two partners should switch roles.

2. At the end of the game, ask students to describe what they have found out about their partners' products, the accuracy of which can be verified by the partner.

3. One possible shortcoming of this activity is that students may tend to read the written information instead of turning it into natural speech. That is why in the alternative procedure, if students are asked to guess what each other's product is, then they have to put away the brochure or information sheet while answering their partner's questions.

Contributor

Wanda Poon is Principal Lecturer in the Division of Humanities and Social Studies at City Polytechnic of Hong Kong.

The Command Game

Levels
Beginning–intermediate

Aims
Generate imperatives
and respond
appropriately to
commands

Class Time
50 minutes

Preparation Time
15–20 minutes

Resources
Slips of paper
Pair of dice (preferably
different colors)

This activity uses imperative structures and combines three language skills—speaking, listening comprehension, and writing—in an atmosphere of cooperation among teammates and competition between teams.

Procedure

1. Introduce the imperative. You may explain it explicitly or you can start by demonstrating.
2. Demonstrate the imperative by having the students, as a group, follow some simple commands. (They may enjoy performing a series of commands such as *stand up, turn around three times, go to the windows, open the windows, shout "banzai" three times . . .*)
3. Prior to playing the Command Game, write 30–40 commands on small slips of paper and put them into an envelope. Also write the word *command* on 8–10 of the slips and include them with the others.
4. Arrange the students in two rows facing each other, six on a side. If there are more than 12 students, the others could be used in supporting roles such as dice roller, timekeeper, and scorekeeper, alternating these jobs with players on the teams. An additional student could be given the task of impartially judging whether or not players abide by the rules of the game. If there are still too many students, two games could be played simultaneously.
5. Roll the dice. If Team A's die shows 3, the third person in line on that team is commander; and if Team B's die shows 4, the fourth person on that team is commandee. The commander takes a command from the envelope (without looking) and reads it to the commandee. The commandee must execute the command satisfactorily to score.

6. Give 5 points for a correct response without help from team members and within 30 seconds; give 3 points for a response without team help within 45 seconds; give 1 point for a response with help from teammates within 1 minute; give no points for no response within 1 minute. (Of course, the point system may be modified to suit your purposes.)
7. If the commander draws one of the 8–10 command slips, that student must make up his or her own imperative on the spot or the team loses a turn.

Caveats and Options

1. After playing 15 minutes or so, have the teams move to opposite sides of the classroom, brainstorm commands, and write them on slips of paper.
2. Encourage students to write outrageous or funny commands, providing they may be followed without injury to life or limb, or embarrassment to any of the students.
3. Play the game again using the imperatives written by students.
4. Include yourself in the process by following commands generated by students.
5. The commandees sometimes have difficulty understanding commands haltingly or ineptly voiced by the commanders. In such cases, you may want to intervene by reading the command yourself. You may wish to invent your own rule or policy to deal with this situation.
6. The game may be shortened or lengthened at your discretion.

Contributor

Randy Smith received an MA in rhetoric at Western Washington University in 1986. He has lived in Japan since November 1989. He currently teaches at the Kobe YMCA.

◆ Vocabulary
Vocabulary Definition Activity

Levels
Low intermediate +

Aims
Practice defining lexical
items in a game context

Class Time
15–45 minutes

Preparation Time
15 minutes

Resources
Chalkboard and chalk
or whiteboard and pen

This activity can be used to practice lexical items recently taught or as a remedial or review activity to be done as a filler. The gamelike context usually attracts students' attention and disguises the fact that this is really a revision and consolidation of lexical items.

Procedure

1. Divide the class into two large groups.
2. Invite one student from one of the groups to come out to the front of the class with his back to the board.
3. Write a word or phrase on the board. (The lexical item should be taken from the day's lesson or a previous lesson.)
4. The members of the student's group then have to define the word on the board without using it in such a way that the student standing near the board can work out what the word is.
5. Set a time limit: 1 minute to score 2 points and 2 minutes to score 1 point. A point can be deducted for giving help (e.g., for saying the first letter or for telling the person how many letters there are in the word/phrase).
6. Give each student in each group a turn to come to the front. The group members not involved sit and watch, while one person keeps the time.
7. Act as arbiter and be firm.

Caveats and Options

1. Some classes prefer the teacher to provide the lexical items, and some are happy to provide their own. Students can often be relied upon to produce the lexical items if they are told where to look (e.g., Units 3, 4, 5 of the coursebook).

2. It is important to confine the source of lexical items to a specific area (e.g., the course syllabus) or students will tend to find as obscure a word as possible from a dictionary and read out a definition without understanding it.
3. Dominant students will tend to speak out more than reticent ones and it is up to the teacher to decide whether to appoint one student to define an item or the whole group.

Contributor

Ron Barnett has taught EFL for more than 10 years in the United Kingdom and the Middle East and is currently working for the British Council in Hong Kong.

Vocabulary List Activity

Levels
Any

Aims
Compile lexical sets
around a heading

Class Time
30–45 minutes

Preparation Time
5–10 minutes

Resources
Chalkboard and chalk
or whiteboard and pen

This activity arouses a lot of interest because all the members of the class can contribute vocabulary items (related to particular topics) in a gamelike atmosphere. This is a good warm-up for speaking, reading, writing, or listening exercises.

Procedure

1. Divide the class into two groups.
2. Toss a coin and ask the winning group if they want to go first or second.
3. Set a time limit (e.g., 1 minute) and write a topic on the board (e.g., six black drinks). The content of the items may be determined by the specific interests of the group or perhaps the content of a course syllabus.
4. Have students from both groups huddle to write their list on paper because there will be bonus points for the group who does not have the first turn.
5. The group who answers first appoints a spokesperson to read their list to you.
6. Write the list on the board and when the requisite number of items has been written—in this case six—decide how many points to award. (Any number less than the requisite can be made up by the other group.)
7. The groups then take turns being first, reading their list so you can write it on the board.
8. When the list is exhausted, have students offer their remaining items.

Caveats and Options

1. Care must be taken to choose topics that are familiar to the learners and culturally appropriate (e.g., not many adolescent Europeans could list six Chinese emperors).
2. Be consistent and firm in arbitrating (e.g., decide beforehand if coffee is a black drink or a dark brown one).
3. With intermediate and more advanced learners, you can add a step in which the students utilize the vocabulary items in written sentences or spoken utterances.

Contributor

Ron Barnett has taught EFL for more than 10 years in the United Kingdom and the Middle East and is currently working for the British Council in Hong Kong.

What Do They Wear?

Levels
Beginning–intermediate

Aims
Generate and practice
specific vocabulary
Acquire cultural
awareness about
clothing and
occupations

Class Time
15–30 minutes

Preparation Time
30 minutes (first time
only)

Resources
Poster paper
Chalkboard and chalk
Magazine pictures of
people from various
occupations (mounted
and then cut in half)

Learners new to a country lack both cultural and linguistic familiarity. This activity lends itself to developing vocabulary about clothing and jobs that students will find useful as they begin their lives in a new country. It also builds an awareness of the occupational fields that may be available to them.

Procedure

1. Lead students to volunteer vocabulary about the different articles of clothing people in the room are wearing. Write the vocabulary on the board.
2. When the list is complete, distribute halves of pictures of people mounted on poster paper (prepared ahead of time).
3. Have each student find the person who has the second half of the picture.
4. Have the students discuss with their partners the clothes the person in the picture is wearing and the job the person probably does.
5. Have each pair present their picture to the rest of the class. Other students can volunteer other ideas about the person's occupation.

Caveats and Options

1. Students can write stories about the lives of the people in their pictures.
2. Once all students have presented their ideas, the class could discuss jobs they might like to do and why.

3. This activity would work well with refugees or high school students in raising their awareness of future job possibilities.

Contributor

Gina Crocetti is completing her MA in TESOL at Portland State University (PSU). She teaches speaking/listening at PSU as well as reading/writing and preliteracy in a program she designed for St. Vincent Hospital.

Real Speak

Levels
Low intermediate +

Aims
Guess the meaning of colloquial and idiomatic speech through context

Class Time
Variable

Preparation Time
Up to 1 hour

Resources
Chalkboard and chalk or equipment to duplicate handouts

Interest in using authentic language in the ESOL classroom is growing. Collecting their own language samples increases the face value of exercises for students, provides a relevant vocabulary list, and encourages the analysis of colloquial language within spoken contexts.

Procedure

1. Have students hand in several samples of spoken language they heard recently but did not understand, along with a few lines from the conversation and/or a short description of the situational context. (Having such context helps in deciphering misheard language samples.)
2. To ease students into the exercise give them an instruction sheet describing types of language items to collect with accompanying examples. Spoken language samples can include idioms (e.g., *hit the sack, piece of cake, hold your horses, under the weather*); slang (*beats me, I'm going to crash, nuke it* [for microwaving]); sayings (e.g., *Let's get this show on the road, Cat's got your tongue*); miscellaneous vocabulary items (e.g., *He is really a character, I outdid myself*), and misheard language (e.g., *My mind was brank* [instead of *blank*], *Ju eat?* for [*Did you eat?*], *festival* [for *first of all*]).
3. Choose appropriate samples for class discussion, typing them on a handout or writing them on the chalkboard.
4. Give small groups of students 20–30 minutes to familiarize themselves with each item on the list and guess its meaning, taking into account the context in which it was heard when such context is given.
5. After reviewing, call on each group to guess the meaning of an item. (Student guessing works best when the teacher pantomimes rather

than talks, signaling students to expand on good guesses or acting out clues.)

6. After the students have done some preliminary guessing, gesture for the student who turned in the language sample to describe the situational context to the class.

7. You will have to talk the students through the exercise the first few times, but be wary of talking too much and taking away students' opportunities to speak. As much as possible, encourage speculation about the language items nonverbally.

Caveats and Options

1. Inevitably, there will be language samples too obscure for students to figure out, although they should be given ample opportunity to guess. In any case, the teacher should make sure all students understand each language sample as the class runs down the list.

2. Students have expressed a great deal of enthusiasm for this exercise. They find the subject matter (i.e., colloquial language) very interesting and are highly motivated to speak in class.

3. The exercise is best done on a regular basis, but it should be noted that it fills up class time quickly. Depending on class length and syllabus needs, you may want to use a few samples each day, or run through a list on a weekly or biweekly basis. Twenty items, along with the group work session, easily occupy two 50-minute class sessions.

4. Students also like to have feedback on every language sample they collect. Because every item is rarely presented for classwide discussion, it is a good idea to give students individual, written feedback on items not covered in class.

5. To build on new vocabulary, ask students to use certain language items in conversation outside of class and report on the reaction they received.

6. Alternately, prior to class, ask an individual student to learn the meaning of a language item he or she handed in, and then have the student act as teacher for that item during class.

7. Real Speak can also be adapted to reading and writing classes by making written material the source for vocabulary items.

Contributors

Lisa Cullen received her MA in TESOL from the Monterey Institute of International Studies and her BFA in Art History from the University of Texas at Austin. She teaches ESL in Davis, California in the United States. John Schillo received his MA in TESOL from the Monterey Institute of International Studies and his BA in Liberal Arts from St. John's College in Santa Fe, New Mexico.

What's Cooking?

Levels
Beginning

Aims
Practice pronunciation
of food-related
vocabulary in a
contextualized and
communicative manner
Express likes and
dislikes
Contrast /l/ and /r/
sounds

Class Time
10 minutes

Preparation Time
None

Resources
Food questionnaire (see
Appendix below)
Large sheets of white
construction or butcher
paper
Crayons or colored
pens

Caveats and Options

Learners are best motivated by activities about their own lives and interests. Because most students enjoy talking about food, this can lead into learning activities that mix authentic speaking situations and high-interest pronunciation practice. Although many students have difficulty contrasting /r/ and /l/ sounds, the food questionnaire format allows them to do so in a low anxiety setting as they question and answer their partners.

Procedure

1. Review pronunciation of all words on the food questionnaire with students, including the concepts of *wonderful, great, pretty good, a little, not really,* and *not at all.*
2. Call attention to the fact that there is either an /r/ or /l/ sound (or both) in each of these words.
3. Begin by asking individual students a question, for example, *How much do you like hamburgers?*
4. Have the students choose their answers from one of the categories mentioned above.
5. Call on volunteers to practice questioning other students in the class.
6. When students are familiar with the questions, have them work with a partner and conduct interviews with the food questionnaire form. Have both partners interview each other. Then reunite the class and question particular partner teams. For example, you can ask, *Elena, how much did Roberto like jello?* Elena would look at her questionnaire in order to give Roberto's response.

1. Have students work in cooperative learning groups to make bar graphs, line graphs, or pie graphs based on one particular question from the food questionnaire. For example, one group may ask students

190

in the entire class what they think of eggs. This can be done by asking a simple question such as, *How do you like eggs?*

2. Based on six possible answers of *wonderful, great, pretty good, a little, not really,* and *not at all,* students can plot the percentages of classmates who feel a particular way about this food.

References and Further Reading

Bowen, J. D. (1972). Contextualizing pronunciation practice in the ESOL classroom. *TESOL Quarterly, 6,* 83-94.

Celce-Murcia, M. (1978). Teaching pronunciation as communication. In J. Morley (Ed.), *Current perspectives on pronunciation* (pp. 1–12). Washington, DC: TESOL.

Pica, T. (1984). Pronunciation activities with an accent on communication. *English Teaching Forum, 22,* 2-6.

Wennerstrom, A. K. (1992). Content-based pronunciation. *TESOL Journal, 1,* 15–18.

continued

Appendix:
Sample Food
Questionnaire

Please interview your partner, asking them what they think of the following foods. For example:

How much do you like _____?
(Pronounced /How much dooyalike/ _____?)

Interviewer's name _____

Interviewee's name _____

Replies: wonderful   great   pretty good
           a little   not really   not at all

Foods:

beans _____

watermelon _____

cookies _____

peas _____

eggs _____

nuts _____

cake _____

hamburgers _____

tacos _____

jello _____

cheese _____

hot dogs _____

ice cream _____

juice _____

corn _____

meat _____

fish _____

soup _____

sandwiches _____

strawberries _____

potato chips _____

milk _____

Contributor

Roseanne Greenfield teaches ESL at the Chinese International School of Hong Kong.

Naming Noun Categories

Levels
Low intermediate +

Aims
Practice naming
members of different
noun categories

Class Time
Variable

Preparation Time
30 minutes

Resources
Index cards

This activity asks learners to assign nouns to appropriate superordinate categories because putting labels on things in the real world is one of the main tasks of language learners. Learning the superordinate terms expands the vocabulary. For example, many students know the word *rice* but may not know the superordinate term *grain*.

Procedure

1. Put students into small groups and have them choose a group leader.
2. Place an index card face down at each group with a noun category on it (e.g., *vegetables*).
3. Say to the groups, "Ready? Go." At this signal have each group leader turn over the card to expose the noun category.
4. Have the groups then come up with a list of five vegetables.
5. Have the group leaders raise their hands as soon their group has five nouns (in this case, vegetable names).
6. Write the lists on the chalkboard, using the superordinate category as the heading (e.g., *vegetables: carrots, peas, beets, onions, cabbage*).
7. Have the students give the names in the plural form. If the student says the singular form, write it on the chalkboard, but after the whole list is on the board, indicate that the list is incorrect and ask the students to monitor their pronunciation of the plural forms.
8. Accept nouns in the students' L1 (e.g., for the categories of vegetables: *zanahorias* [the Spanish word for *carrots*]) but require the students to find the English equivalent. (If there is no equivalent, accept the item as it is given in the L1 and write it on the chalkboard.)
9. The first group to compile a correct list wins the round and gets two points. If the list is incorrect, call on the group who was second,

and so forth. (In case of a tie, where the groups have correct lists, each group receives 2 points.)

10. At the end of the exercise, the group with the highest number of points wins.

Caveats and Options

1. Use more than one category of noun at a time, by giving each group three cards with different categories. As soon as a group has come up with all items within the categories, have group leaders raise their hands to signal completion of the task.
2. Reverse the process by giving the groups cards containing a list of things (e.g., _____: wheat, oats, rice, barley, sorghum) and asking students to come up with the category.
3. Suggested superordinate terms include: *fruits, grains, farm animals, dogs, cats, birds, fish, tools, automobiles, furniture, tableware, buildings, occupations, meats, cheeses, metals, beverages, dances, vehicles, professions, gases, trees, flowers, modes of transportation, electrical appliances, items of clothing.*
4. Where appropriate, more difficult categories may be used, such as types of governments.

Contributor

Ted Plaister taught in the Department of ESL, University of Hawaii for 24 years. He has also taught in Thailand, Japan, Micronesia, and American Samoa.

Kanji Translations Into English

Levels
High
beginning–intermediate;
Japanese speakers

Aims
Working together to
describe Kanji symbols
in English

Class Time
50–90 minutes

Preparation Time
20 minutes

Resources
Paper and pencils
Dictionaries (Japanese/
English and Japanese)
Sample Kanji Language
Handout (see Appendix
below)

This activity provides Japanese students with a purpose for using English, by encouraging them to produce meaningful interactions as they work out the meaning of their names and them from Kanji to English.

Procedure

1. Pair off students and make sure each pair has the necessary dictionaries.
2. Demonstrate the activity by asking a student to come to the chalkboard and write his/her first name vertically in Kanji. Encourage everyone to help the student work out and explain the meaning of the name (e.g., an arrow of peace) in English, while you make notes and write the determined meaning on the chalkboard.
3. Because Kanji does not always have a meaning, encourage students to give some personal background about how they got their names (e.g., Who chose their name?).
4. In pairs, have the students work out the meaning of their names with the help of dictionaries.
5. Give the language handout to the pairs (see Appendix below), and have them use some of the phrases to stimulate conversation about the Kanji.
6. Walk around the classroom and clarify vocabulary and language problems for students.
7. Have the students change partners and exchange the meaning of their name and their background information in English with others.

Caveats and Options

1. Have groups of four work out a Kanji for your name, by writing your name on the chalkboard and helping students with vocabulary. Have one person from each group write the Kanji for your name on the board and give an explanation in English.

Appendix: Sample Kanji Language Handout

2. Although this lesson is directed at Japanese students, it could be adapted to a variety of students from different language backgrounds.

Here are some questions and answers you may choose from to help in your discussions of Kanji with your partners.

Question phrases:

- What's *ken* (syllable)?
- What does *ken* mean?
- Who gave you your name (parents/grandparents)?
- Why did your parents want to name you _____?
- Do you like your name?
- Do you want to change your name?

Answer phrases:

- I think it means . . .
- This Kanji has three meanings.
- I think my name means . . .
- I think so too . . . /I don't think so. I think it means . . .
- My name has no meaning. I think this is a luck Kanji.
- This Kanji has a good sound to it.
- My grandfather/grandmother liked _____ so they named me_____ .
- My [relative] thought it's a lucky Kanji.
- The number of strokes/lines in the Kanji makes it lucky.
- I like your name.
- I think you are like your name./I think your name suits you.
- You are really like your name (sweet, pretty . . .).

Contributor

Roshani SenGupta teaches English at the Kobe YMCA College, Kobe, Japan.

Part III: Pronunciation

◆ Segmental Phonemes
Wending Your Way Through the Language Lab

Levels
Any

Aims
Use self-access
pronunciation
improvement
audiotapes effectively
Discover which
pronunciation points
need practice and how
to prioritize practice

Class Time
None

Preparation Time
1–12 hours (depending
on the number of L1s
represented in the
class)

Resources
Reference works
Paper and pen, or word
processor
Photocopy or ditto
machine

This activity promotes pronunciation improvement through independent study. Though they may receive some diagnostic evaluation of
their pronunciation difficulties, many students do not know which of their
problems can be addressed independently with audiotapes in the language
laboratory. Also, students often are unable to prioritize their independent
pronunciation work because they are unaware of which pronunciation
difficulties affect their intelligibility the most. If the language laboratory
has many tape sets for pronunciation work, students may not be familiar
enough with the material to determine which ones correspond to their
needs. However, if supplied with a guide sheet outlining which pronunciation difficulties need immediate attention and which audiotapes offer the
necessary practice, learners can approach independent study effectively.

Procedure

Create log sheets for each student using the following guidelines.

1. Look up the L1 of the student(s) in a reference work. Write Word
   Stress as the first category if it is listed as a problem for students
   with this L1. Put a box after Word Stress. Put a line after the box.
   Leave space for comments before writing the next category.
2. Write Sentence Stress as the second category, if it is listed as a
   problem for students with this L1. List any subcategories of sentence
   stress (e.g., blending, rhythm) under the category. Put a box and a
   line after each category and subcategory listed. Leave space for
   comments or additions.

3. Write Intonation as the third category, if it is listed as a problem for learners from this L1. Continue with subcategories and specific intonation patterns with boxes and lines after each as described in Step 2.

4. List Consonants and Vowels as the last category. Write each contrast or difficulty listed in the reference work with a box and line after each one. Leave space for comments and additions.

5. If creating guide sheets for more than one L1, code this master sheet so that it can easily be differentiated from others and referred to for future classes. For example, type Korean in the corner of the sheet.

6. Repeat the procedure for each L1 of the students in your class.

7. Copy as many sheets for each L1 as there are students in the class who speak that L1. File the master sheets for future use.

8. Write each student's name and date at the top of a sheet. Mark the boxes of each feature that specific students need to work on.

9. On the line after each box that is marked, indicate which materials the individual student should use by writing the name(s), title(s) of tape program(s), number(s), or side(s) of the tape(s) in the laboratory. In the space in each category, write in any problems or areas of work that the student needs to address in addition to those on the master sheet.

10. Number each marked feature so that the student knows which to work on first, second, and so on.

11. Hand out the guide sheets to students in class. For questions about the guide sheets, set aside class time or office hours.

Caveats and Options

1. If the class is small enough or if language laboratory work is required, have students sign up for conferences. Go over the guide sheet, laboratory procedures, work assignments, and priorities with individual students.

2. Preparation time is greatly reduced after the first master sheets are created. The time will vary with each instructional term depending on how many students are in the class and how many different L1s are represented.

3. Keep copies of the students' individual guide sheets to help them document their progress.

References and Further Reading

Swan, M., & Smith, B. (Eds). (1987). *Learner English: A teacher's guide to interference and other problems*. Cambridge: Cambridge University Press.

Kenworthy, J. (1987). *Teaching English pronunciation*. London: Longman.

Contributor

Beverly J. Beisbier, Instructor at the University of California, Berkeley Extension, has developed ESOL courses and materials and taught in the United States and France.

Pronunciation Warm Up

Levels
Any; adolescents and
adults

Aims
Prepare vocal apparatus
for clarity, comfort, and
strength in speaking
Relax and relieve
tension related to oral
production
Enhance muscle
extension and flexibility
and control breathing

Class Time
10–15 minutes/warm-
up session
20–30 minutes for
explanations

Preparation Time
None

Resources
None required, music
helpful

Learning to speak another language requires different movements of the cheeks, jaw, lips, tongue, teeth, glottis, and lungs. Gaining control of and flexibility with one's physical speaking apparatus facilitates changes in accent and voice quality and enhances overall oral production.

Procedure

1. In a relaxed and confident manner, lead students through the following exercise sequence:

   - Stand with feet shoulder-width apart.
   - Extend arms to side and shake loosely from the shoulders.
   - Bend over from the waist, exhale, hang. Come up, inhale, stretch arms to ceiling.
   - Loosen chest and abdomen and breath deeply.
   - Roll and loosen shoulders, and rotate head gently in a big circle.

2. Breathe deeply while loosening and relaxing body by concentrating on one area at a time:

a. arms	g. back of head	l. nose
b. shoulders	h. ears	m. cheeks
c. back	i. top of head	n. jaw
d. abdomen	j. forehead, temple	o. lips
e. chest	k. eyes	p. tongue
f. neck		

3. "Wake up" by yawning a big "Aaaaah!" Stretch your mouth: first your whole mouth, then one side at a time.
4. Stretch your mouth from side to side, up, down, forward, back, around and around. Make funny faces.

5. Loosen your cheeks manually. Massage your cheeks, jaw, chin. Inhale and exhale, saying "Blah blah blah" loosely.
6. Loosen lips manually. Inhale and exhale by vibrating your lips against each other.
7. Waggle your tongue in and out, hitting your teeth. Keep your lips relaxed.
8. Vocalize vowel sounds at a comfortable pitch, using a full breath. Focus on the position of your jaw, tongue, and lips. Make the sounds in this order:

    a. /i/   b. /e/   c. /a/   d. /o/   e. /u/

9. Vocalize vowel sounds again, shifting from one vowel to another. Close your eyes and concentrate on the following sequence of feeling the jaw, tongue, and lips in position and as they move.

    a. /i/ — /a/
    b. /i/ — /u/
    c. /a/ — /i/
    d. /a/ — /u/
    e. /i/ — /a/ — /u/

Caveats and Options

1. Draw parallels (or, better, elicit them from students) between warming up and performing in other fields, such as music (e.g., piano scales, vocal exercises) and sports (e.g., lifting weights for baseball, hitting balls against a backboard for tennis). Point out that learning to speak in a foreign language requires changes in the use of one's physical speaking apparatus.
2. Introduce vocabulary as needed. Some useful phrases include the following: *breathe deeply, take a deep breath, inhale, exhale, tense, relax, stretch, hang, separate, vibrate, waggle, relaxation, stress, tension, worries, cares, muscles, back, shoulders, chest, abdomen, neck, head, forehead, eyes, nose, cheeks, jaw, lips, tongue, teeth, loosely, gently, peacefully, slowly.*
3. Explain which parts of the body you're going to have the students try to relax, and which muscles you'll have them tense and flex afterwards. Play some peaceful music. Have the students put down

their pens and books and remove restraining outer garments if temperature permits.
4. Be sure to practice a routine before trying it with students so that you can perform with confidence. Develop various routines. Have fun working out and warming up.

Contributor

Marsha Chan teaches ESL at Mission College in Santa Clara, California. She has published a book and videotapes on pronunciation and authored articles on oral communication. This routine is based on her Pronunciation Workout for Foreign Language Learners, *a videotape production for teacher education and classroom use.*

Minimal Pairs

Levels
Any

Aims
Perceive and pronounce
difficult pairs of
phonemes

Class Time
5–10 minutes

Preparation Time
10 minutes

Resources
Chalkboard (or large
cards) and chalk (or
markers)
Lists of minimal pairs

This teaching technique is very handy when presenting difficult pronunciation items. I have used this many times when trying to help students grapple with the difference between confusing pairs (e.g., *-teen* vs. *-ty* or *sheep* vs. *ship*).

Procedure

1. Write two groups of minimal pairs on the board. For example, if you are practicing the *-teen* versus *-ty* distinction, write the numbers 13–19 on one side of the board and the numbers 30, 40, 50, 60, 70, 80, and 90 on the other side of the board. Label the left group with a large A and the right group with a large B. (Another grouping could be the distinction between /i/ and /ɪ/, as in *sheep*, *cheap*, *feet*, and *ship*, *chip*, *fit.*)
2. Demonstrate by saying any of the numbers on the board. The students have to say A or B to indicate which group the word (sound) is in. Cover your mouth with a sheet of paper so that students cannot rely on any visual clues, or turn away from the class as you say the words to make it seem more challenging.
3. Once the students understand the system, have them take turns calling out a word to see if listeners recognize it as the speaker's intended word. (You may want to have students write down the word and the code—A or B—before they say it in order to check whether the student actually pronounced the word correctly.)

Caveats and Options

1. Have students work in groups of four.
2. The first student must write down a word and then say the word.
3. The other students each say which group they have heard (A or B).

4. Students receive 1, 2, or 3 points according to how many of the other group members were able to identify the intended word.

Contributor

Keith S. Folse is the Educational Director at the Language Academy in Maebashi, Japan.

The Restaurant Menu

Levels
Beginning

Aims
Practice auditory
discrimination of food
words with easily
confused vowel sounds

Class Time
15 minutes

Preparation Time
None

Resources
Paper and pencil
Sample menu (see
Appendix)

Restaurant menus are useful sources of language for real-life tasks. Using learning groups to categorize easily confused vowel sounds on restaurant menus gives students a chance to discriminate between and practice these sounds with immediate feedback from their peers. The competitive nature of a round table activity is a good team builder and offers positive social rewards for participation in pronunciation.

Procedure

1. Have students review words on the sample menu together and with you.
2. Place special emphasis on the difference in pronunciation between the /e/ and /ɛ/ sounds.
3. Divide the class into cooperative groups of four to work on the categorizing words on the menu by sound. All four students in the group will work on one sheet of paper while taking turns answering individually in a clockwise motion.
4. The first student makes a column for the /e/ words and picks one at random, such as *grapes* or *steak.*
5. After writing *and* speaking the word, the first student passes the paper clockwise to the next student, who will choose another /e/ word like *pancake* or *potato.*
6. If the next student cannot think of a word, teammates may offer suggestions, as long as the intended student does the actual writing of the word.
7. After all the /e/ words are exhausted, have the students make another column for the /ɛ/ words and continue answering in a clockwise manner.

8. When all groups are finished, make a master list of each category on the board by asking the different groups to supply the answers out loud. In this manner, all groups can check their own lists against those on the chalkboard.

Caveats and Options

1. Explain food items on the menu and review pronunciation.
2. Introduce a few simple questions and answers about ordering in a restaurant. For example:

   Q: Are you ready to order?
   A: Yes, I'd like . . .
   Q: What would you like to drink?
   A: I'd like . . .
   Q: What would you like for dinner?
   Q: What would you like for breakfast?
   Q: Would you like soup?
   Q: Would you like salad?
   Q: Would you like anything else?
   A: No, thank you.

3. Put students in cooperative learning groups. Give and take orders from the menu until everyone is comfortable with the words.
4. Then ask for volunteer groups to come to the front of the class and present their orders, giving or taking.
5. Have students role-play by setting tables, bringing in real food, and simulating a restaurant in class.
6. Students can also discuss prices and write them on their own menus.

Appendix:
Sample Menu

Menu

Soups
1. Baked red bean soup
2. Bacon vegetable soup

Salads
1. Celery and lettuce on a plate
2. Salad with pepper dressing
3. Grape, raisin, and mango salad

Dinner
1. Pepper steak and french fries
2. Egg roll and vegetables
3. Spaghetti and fresh baked bread

Breakfast
1. Pancakes and grape jelly
2. Bacon and eggs
3. Strawberries and mango on a plate

Desserts
1. Cherry cupcakes
2. Lemon cake
3. Strawberry sundae

Extras
1. Raisin bread
2. Potato chips
3. Extra jelly

Drinks
1. Grapefruit juice
2. Lemonade
3. Strawberry shake

Contributor

Roseanne Greenfield teaches ESL at the Chinese International School of Hong Kong.

What Time?

Levels
Beginning

Aims
Contrast the /č/ and /š/
sounds in time-related
vocabulary
Practice reduced form
phrases, rhythm, and
stress in asking
questions

Class Time
15 minutes

Preparation Time
None

Resources
What Time? Worksheet
(see Appendix below)
Pictures of people from
magazines

The transfer of pronunciation skills from controlled practice to free speech is an important goal for L2 learners. Practicing the /č/ and /š/ sounds in simple reduced-form questions found in daily conversation will reinforce spontaneous and natural sounding communication. A thematic unit such as What Time? offers an excellent vehicle for real-life dialogue that incorporates target sounds as well as the natural rhythm and stress involved in asking questions.

Procedure

1. Practice pronouncing vocabulary words with students before starting the activity.
2. Practice asking the following questions in reduced form with the class:

   - When are you going to wash your hands?
     (pronounced "Whenerya gonna wash yer hands?")
   - When are you going to watch the movie?
     (pronounced "Whenerya gonna watch the movie?")

3. Give each student a copy of the What Time? Worksheet.
4. Have the students cut out the small clocks and paste them on the right side of their questions in order to form answers. For example, if you paste the 4:00 clock face next to Question 1 ("When are you going to wash your face?"), the answer is "at 4:00."
5. Next, have students pair off and interview their partners, writing down their partner's answer next to that of their own.
6. When the interviews have been completed, ask individual students about their own or their partner's answers.

Caveats and Options

1. Make alternative What Time? Worksheets with other categories (e.g., errands to do, classes to attend).

2. Develop past tense worksheets using questions beginning with *When did you . . . ?* (pronounced as "Whendidja . . . ?").

3. Have individual students act out vocabulary words in front of class, while the remaining students guess the words and pronounce them out loud.

4. Give cooperative learning groups one picture of an unknown individual. Each group must write a short paragraph about the daily routine of their individual, utilizing contrasting /č/ and /š/ vocabulary words and times of the day. This exercise can also be done as a whole-class activity in which students contribute their ideas orally as you write them on the board.

5. Scramble the students' paragraphs containing embedded vocabulary words and cut them into five or six parts. Give each group a different scrambled paragraph and ask them to reassemble the parts, later reading them back to the original group when they are finished.

6. Give each student an index card with one of the target vocabulary words. Have the students stand up and circulate around the class, asking at least 15 other students the question *What did you do this morning?* (Pronounced "Whadidja do this morning?") Each student responds using the word on the index card. Example: (Face) *I washed my face this morning.* Extra words (such as *chop, shave, change clothes, share, shout, shoes, chair, cheated, channel, chat, check, chess, children, chose, shrimp, shrink,* and *shorts*) can be added to the list.

Appendix: What Time? Worksheet

Practice pronouncing the following vocabulary words:

wash	watch	brush	church	sandwich
finish	shirt	couch	shop	catch
lunch	shower	show		

Now practice asking:

When are you going to wash your hands?
(Pronounced /Whenerya gonna wash your hands/?)

When are you going to finish your dinner?
(Pronounced /Whenerya gonna finish your dinner/?)

Cut out the clocks and paste them next to each question as an answer:

1. When are you going to wash your face?
2. When are you going to watch the movies?
3. When are you going to brush your teeth?
4. When are you going to go to church?
5. When are you going to eat your sandwich?
6. When are you going to finish your work?
7. When are you going to clean your shirt?
8. When are you going to watch TV on the couch?
9. When are you going to shop for food?
10. When are you going to catch the bus?
11. When are you going to eat lunch?
12. When are you going to take a shower?
13. When are you going to show me your bike?

Contributor

Roseanne Greenfield teaches ESL at the Chinese International School of Hong Kong.

Large-Group Interviews

Levels
Beginning

Aims
Contrast the /č/ and /š/ sounds found in time-related vocabulary
Practice reduced-form phrases

Class Time
30 minutes

Preparation Time
None

Resources
TV Schedule Worksheet (see Appendix below)

It is easy for students to speak about their leisure time activities such as watching TV. Thus, large-group interviews about TV viewing and scheduling allow students to practice contrasting target sounds in a student-centered learning environment. Large-group interviews also offer multisensory lessons for various styles including physical activity, listening practice, and social interaction.

Procedure

1. Practice reading the names of television shows listed on the TV Schedule Worksheet.
2. Discuss what each show is about, who in the class has actually seen these shows, and what time they air in real life.
3. Then practice the following model questions with students:

   Q: What time should we watch "Charlie Brown?"
   A: Let's watch it at 6:00.
   Q: What time should we watch "The Lucy Show?"
   A: Let's watch it at 6:30.

4. Have students first work in small groups to decide the times they (as a group) will watch the following shows.

   - One student asks the other students, "What time should we watch the _____ show?"
   - The other students decide, and everyone writes down the same answer on each of their papers.
   - A second student asks the second question, and everyone in the group decides the answer together.

5. Students continue asking questions and making decisions in a clockwise direction until all of the group's answers have been written down.
6. After each group has completed their own schedule, give students a fresh TV Schedule Worksheet and have them practice the following questions:

A: What time do you watch "The Lucy Show?"
B: We watch "The Lucy Show" at 8:00.
A: What time do you watch Channel 3 cartoons?
B: We watch Channel 3 cartoons at 7:30.

7. Then have students walk around the room, talking to other students who are not in their group, finding out what time other groups have decided to watch various shows. When all schedules have been filled out, have students report back to their original group.
8. Ask questions about the survey results.

Caveats and Options

1. An alternative TV Schedule Worksheet can be devised using English language radio or television broadcasts in your area.
2. Other categories can be used to fill in a weekday schedule (e.g., classes to attend, places to visit while sightseeing).

Continued

Appendix: Sample TV Schedule Worksheet

Practice the following questions and answers:

A: What time do you watch The Lucy Show?
B: I watch The Lucy Show at 8:00.

A: What time do you watch Channel 3 Cartoons?
B. I watch Channel 3 Cartoons at 7:30.

Walk around the room and talk to students who are not in your group. Find out what time they watch all of the shows below. Put the name of the show and their name on the two blank lines:

Weekday Schedule

2:00	_____	_____	*The Lucy Show*
2:30	_____	_____	*Star Search*
3:00	_____	_____	*Channel 9 Sports*
3:30	_____	_____	*Showtime*
4:00	_____	_____	*Channel 7 News*
4:30	_____	_____	*Cheers*
5:00	_____	_____	*Bewitched*
5:30	_____	_____	*The Fishing Show*
6:00	_____	_____	*Charlie Brown*
6:30	_____	_____	*The Muppet Show*
7:00	_____	_____	*The Cosby Show*
7:30	_____	_____	*Channel 3 Cartoons*
8:00	_____	_____	
8:30	_____	_____	
9:00	_____	_____	
9:30	_____	_____	
10:00	_____	_____	
10:30	_____	_____	

Contributor

Roseanne Greenfield teaches ESL at the Chinese International School of Hong Kong.

Bingo

Levels
Any

Aims
Practice with the /Θ/,
/δ/ and /s/ sounds
Discriminate auditory
differences in street
names

Class Time
45 minutes

Preparation Time
None

Resources
Bingo card
Double-spaced list of
street names from map
(see the following
activity, Minimal Pairs
with Street Names)

Learners make the most progress when they actively monitor their own pronunciation and sound discrimination abilities. Bingo is an ideal way to focus on contrasting sounds of street names in an enjoyable context. Because many street names utilized in this exercise are very similar, the speaker's pronunciation accuracy must be relatively high in order to ensure accurate communication. Students must actively concentrate on the sounds being produced by their peers, and speakers must actively monitor their own pronunciation.

Procedure

1. Ask students to originate names of streets, directions, and locations for the card and from the worksheet.
2. Write names on the board as students call them out.
3. After compiling a list of 25–30 names, pass out empty bingo sheets and have the students fill in the grid boxes at random to use as their game cards.
4. Begin the game by calling out names on the board while students mark their cards with markers by using beans, bingo chips, or small bits of colored paper.
5. Next, ask a volunteer to be the "word caller." (This gives individuals practice in pronunciation, while the rest of the class receives practice in auditory discrimination.)
6. Cut up the list of the street names and place all street names in a hat, allowing many students to select and then read out loud the names they have chosen.

Caveats and Options

1. You can also allow students to cut up the list of street names from the Map Worksheet (see Appendix in next activity, Minimal Pairs

216

With Street Names) to make bingo cards themselves, rather than having students originate their own words.

2. If this is the case, use the list of street names from the Map Worksheet for auditory discrimination practice by asking students to cut out particular words one at a time before pasting them on the bingo board. For example, say: "Please cut out Cassy Street. Now cut out Norse Street."

3. Students then place these words at random on their game board.

Contributor

Roseanne Greenfield teaches ESL at the Chinese International School of Hong Kong.

Minimal Pairs With Street Names

Levels
Any

Aims
Practice /Θ/, /δ/, and /s/
sounds
Practice discriminating
differences in street
names with similar
sounds

Class Time
10 minutes

Preparation Time
None

Resources
Map Worksheet (see
Appendix below)

The /Θ/, /δ/ and /s/ sounds are among the most difficult for L2 speakers to produce. Giving directions with minimal pair street names offers a learning activity with an abundance of lexical items using these target sounds. Having students simulate a meaningful real-life situation also helps develop skills that can later extend beyond the classroom environment.

Procedure

1. Practice pronouncing names of streets with the class.
2. Put similar sounding street names on the board (such as Cassy Street/ Cathy Street) with the numerals 1 and 2 above each respective word.
3. Say one of the two words.
4. Ask students to tell you if they heard Number 1 or 2. Beginning students can signal by holding up either one or two fingers or by saying the word.
5. Next, ask individual volunteers to come up to the front and pronounce one of the two similar sounding street names by themselves.

Caveats and Options

This activity can provide practice in preparation for the following activity, called Giving Directions.

Appendix:
Sample Map
Worksheet

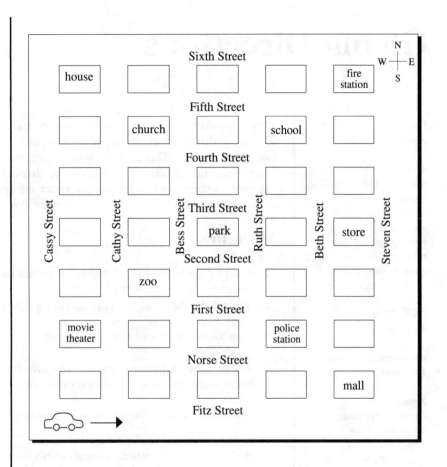

Contributor

Roseanne Greenfield teaches ESL at the Chinese International School of Hong Kong.

Giving Directions

Levels
Intermediate +

Aims
Contrast /Θ/, /δ/, and /s/
sounds
Order directions in
sequence
Practice giving and
receiving directions in a
contextualized and
communicative manner

Class Time
45 minutes

Preparation Time
15 minutes

Resources
Giving Directions
Worksheet (see
Appendix below)
Map Worksheet (see
previous activity,
Minimal Pairs With
Street Names)
Overhead projector
(OHP), OHP
transparency of the
map, if possible

There is often more than one way to arrive at a particular destination, making direction giving an ideal way to practice the repetition of contrasting sounds. This activity also simulates meaningful and realistic conversational situations in which the direction giver must order, sequence, gesture, and communicate exact information clearly and succinctly. It is a challenge that most students enjoy.

Procedure

1. Practice the following dialogue on giving directions together with the class (see Appendix).
2. Explain the different ways of describing how you can get to the same place.
3. Display the overhead transparency of the street map or refer to the paper copy.
4. Ask students a question such as, *How do I get to the school?*
5. Let students tell you the answer(s) as you write them down on the board.
6. Do this for several locations. For example:

   A: How do I get to the school?
   B: Go east on Fitz Street, then go north on Ruth Street, and then go east again on Fourth Street. The school is on the corner of Fourth and Ruth.
   A: How do I get to the store?
   B: Go north on Cassy Street, then go east on First Street, and then go north on Beth Street. The store is on the corner of Beth and Second.

Caveats and Options

1. Students can work together with partners to give directions to the places listed on the Giving Directions Worksheet (see Appendix). This is a fairly difficult exercise and may take more time than usual.
2. When students are finished working with partners, ask volunteer pairs to come up and demonstrate giving directions.
3. You may also ask one volunteer to give directions and another to point out the route on the OHP.
4. Have the students apply this knowledge by giving their partner directions to their own homes or to a location in their own city.

Appendix: Giving Directions Worksheet

Practice the following examples:

1. You are starting from the house

   A: Excuse me. How do I get to the police station from here?
   B: Go east on Fifth Street, then go south on Beth Street, and then go west on Norse Street. The police station is on the corner of Norse and Beth.

2. You are at the park
   A: Excuse me. How do I get to the movie theater from here?
   B: Go west on Second Street and then go south on Cassy Street. The movie theater is on the corner of Cassy and First.

Work with partners to give directions to the following places:

1. You are at the fire station
   A: Excuse me. How do I get to the zoo from here?
2. You are at the movie theater
   A: Excuse me. How do I get to the church from here?
3. You are at the church
   A: Excuse me. How do I get to the fire station from here?
4. You are at the mall
   A: Excuse me. How do I get to the house from here?
5. You are at the school
   A: Excuse me. How do I get to the mall from here?

6. You are at the park
   A: Excuse me. How do I get to the police station from here?
7. You are at the school
   A: Excuse me. How do I get to the mall from here?
8. You are at the store
   A: Excuse me. How do I get to the zoo from here?
9. You are at the mall
   A: Excuse me. How do I get to the church from here?

Contributor

Roseanne Greenfield teaches ESL at the Chinese International School of Hong Kong.

Wascal Wabbit

Levels
Any; Japanese speakers

Aims
Improve pronunciation
of /l/ and /r/ phonemes

Class Time
20 minutes

Preparation Time
None

Resources
None

English has four continuant phonemes: /r/, /l/, /j/, and /w/. Although many languages have a similar number (or more), Japanese has one less. Only a single phoneme (somewhat closer to [r]) subsumes both the /r/ and the /l/ of English. To overcome this problem, I developed the Wascal Wabbit technique, which depends on two facts about English pronunciation. First, English [l] actually has two allophones: (a) clear (light) *l* and (b) dark *l*. Dark l is also called *velar l*. The word *little* uses both allophones (the second *l* is a velar *l*). Second, for many English speakers, only the trill of the tongue separates [r] (trilled) from [w] (not trilled). Frequently, even young native speakers of English cannot accurately trill the [r]. These children consistently pronounce [w] for /r/. Elmer Fudd, a character from the Bugs Bunny cartoons, also pronounces it this way, calling Bugs "you wascally wabbit." By associating /l/ with velarized [l] and by emulating Elmer Fudd, the students can distinguish the English phonemes /l/ and /r/.

Procedure

1. Start this lesson with a Bugs Bunny cartoon, preferably one in which Elmer Fudd does a fair amount of speaking (my particular favorite is "The Rabbit of Seville").
2. Then, throughout the lesson, velarize all of your [l]s.
3. After the cartoon, inform the students that, for the day, they will separate their /r/ and /l/s.
4. Then begin the next section in the text (unrelated to pronunciation) and follow your regular lesson plan.
5. Write the letters R and L very large as column headings large in the center of the board. Put the word *little* underneath the L, and the phrase *rascal rabbit* with the Rs crossed off and W written above each one under the R heading.

6. Demonstrate the pronunciation of the words in both columns and have a few students try to pronounce them.
7. Demonstrate velarized [l] clearly and give a few more samples.
8. Ask all of the students to speak like Elmer Fudd. Start with a few lines from the cartoon and then conduct most of the class pronouncing /r/ as [w].
9. As the class nears the end, try a few pronunciation drills.
10. Once again, describe the [r] as nearly identical to the [w] (i.e., fronted) and the velar [l] (i.e., backed).
11. Give the students a list of words with both /r/ and /l/ (e.g., *learn, pearl, wriggle, rail, large, roll, lord*, and a few others). These words do not have to be vocabulary words.
12. Pronounce each word slowly and clearly. Place special emphasis on the moving of the tongue to the velar for the /l/ and forward and trilling for the /r/.
13. Read the list again but with one different student repeating each word after you. Carefully correct the pronunciation of each student.
14. Once the students can hear and identify the difference between the two sounds, assign the list as homework. Have the students practice the list, listening for the difference in sounds and remembering the difference between backed and fronted sounds.

Caveats and Options

1. Tell students only that many learners of English have difficulties with these sounds and that this lesson is just to help head off any difficulty they will have in the future. (That is, never destroy the students' confidence over a minor deficiency they may be aware of and comfortable with.)
2. A few gentle reminders to the students will keep them pronouncing /r/ as [w]. The first students using [r] are called *wascally wabbits*, we all have a bit of a laugh, and then I continue the class with the other activity.
3. In the next class, ask the students to pronounce one word each from the list. A quick review of a few pronunciations is normally required, but the majority of the students have already acquired knowledge of the difference. In later classes, an occasional drill, complete with "wascal wabbit" is conducted. For new vocabulary,

the difference of [l] versus [r] pronunciation must be emphasized for a few weeks. Most of the students are amazed at how clear the difference becomes. Once established and incorporated into new vocabulary items, this difference becomes a self-sustaining one.

4. The Wascal Wabbit technique works because the students are provided with an associated distinction on which to separate two phonemes that are not distinguished in their L1s. The students may not sound like native speakers; nonetheless, the improvement is quite remarkable. First, the analogy is the acquisition, then the analogy aids the acquisition.

Contributor   *Joseph J. J. Hantsch is an instructor at Trident College in Nagoya, Japan. He did graduate work in linguistics at the University of Chicago.*

Who and What Do You Love?

Levels
Low
intermediate–advanced

Aims
Practice pronunciation
of consonant and vowel
pairs
Work cooperatively in
order to solve a logic
puzzle

Class Time
30–40 minutes

Preparation Time
20 minutes

Resources
Sample Worksheet (see
Appendix below)
Clues cut into strips

In pronunciation classes, much time is spent on choral repetition of minimal pairs or on pair work in which one of the students enunciates a particular word or sound and the other student determines the sound or the word heard. Although these techniques are valuable, they may not help students realize that the sounds they pronounce adequately in isolation may not be pronounced as well when the stress is on meaning, not form. Moreover, pure practice can be a bit boring for the students, causing them to lose their motivation for improvement. The following exercise addresses the above problems by allowing the students to practice their pronunciation while working together communicatively to solve a logic problem.

Procedure

1. Preteach the difficult vocabulary and review the target sounds before starting the puzzle.
2. Organize the students into small groups.
3. Distribute the clues to the students. If there are too many clues for the number of students, disperse them to the groups at random so that some students have two and some have only one.
4. Tell the students to speak English only. They may write notes and use the grid as provided. They may ask their partners to repeat the clue as many times as they wish. They may not ask their partner to show them the clue or spell a word for them.
5. Have students compare their answers across the groups. Here are the answers.

   Reedy—Murray—Tennis
   Leedy—Maury—Shopping
   Welsh—Lilly—Movies

Wersh—Mary—Swimming
Walsh—Molly—Reading

6. Where there are differences of opinion, have the students explain their logic.

Caveats and Options

1. You should complete the puzzle before giving it to the students.
2. You can create many different puzzles on this model by utilizing different problematic phonemes.
3. Advanced students can design their own puzzles in pairs or small groups and then challenge their classmates with those puzzles.

Appendix: Sample Worksheet

Five people are sitting and chatting in a cafe. They are: Walsh, Wersh, Leedy, Reedy, and Welsh. They all have wives or husbands: Molly, Mary, Maury, Murray, and Lilly. They also have different hobbies: movies, tennis, swimming, shopping, and reading. Your job is to read the clue(s) you have to your partners and to listen to your partner's clues. Find out who the husbands and wives are, and what the hobbies of Walsh, Wersh, Leedy, Reedy and Welsh are. Each person has only one mate and one hobby. You can write notes and/or use the grid below. You cannot ask how to spell a name. You can ask as many times as you like for your partners to repeat a clue—as long as you do so in English. You may also discuss your strategies with your partners—as long as you do it in English. Have fun!

Clues

- My name is Reedy. Mary's husband's hobby isn't reading, but Maury's wife likes to go shopping.
- My name is Leedy. Welsh's wife is Lilly. As for me, I'm not at all good at sports.
- My name is Welsh. Those who like sports are Murray's wife and Wersh.
- My name is Wersh. My wife is not Maury. I like sports very much.
- My name is Walsh. I love reading. Reedy is crazy about tennis.

	Murray	Maury	Lilly	Mary	Molly
Reedy					
Leedy					
Welsh					
Wersh					
Walsh					

	Movies	Tennis	Swim	Shop	Read
Reedy					
Leedy					
Welsh					
Wersh					
Walsh					

Contributor

Robert M. Homan is an instructor at the International Christian University in Tokyo, Japan. He edited a special issue of JALT Language Teacher in which cooperative language learning was the main focus.

Sound and Rhythm Orchestra

Levels
Beginning +

Aims
Practice producing
problematic sounds,
such as consonant
clusters
Practice rhythm in
speech

Class Time
15 minutes

Preparation Time
5–10 minutes

Resources
Overhead projector
(OHP) and
transparencies

In this activity, students create a sound and rhythm orchestra by chorally chanting a combination of different rhythmic sound patterns. The activity removes the learners' focus from lexical, syntactic, morphological, and discourse issues to concentrate entirely on phonology. It can be a fun (and funny) way of getting students to practice difficult sounds in the target language.

Procedure

1. Elicit the meaning of *orchestra*.
2. Tell the students that they are going to form their own orchestra.
3. Divide the class into six groups of students.
4. Assign one rhythmic sound pattern (see Step 8 below) to each of the groups. (These patterns will have been selected to give practice in the particular sound production problems of the class.)
5. Write these sound patterns on a transparency with the stressed sounds underlined.
6. Model the sound pattern in a lively, rhythmic manner.
7. Have each group echo the utterance chorally four or five times.
8. Choose from the following patterns:

   - *toodle* oodle oodle, *toodle* ta *to*
   - *boom* boody *boom* boody *boom boom boom*
   - *wee wee* widdly widdly *wee*
   - zizzy *zan* zizzy *zan* zizzy *zan zan* zizzy
   - plip *plop* plip *plop* plippity plippity *plop*
   - rippity *roo* rippity *roo* rippity rippity *roo*

9. Give the students enough time to master their own particular rhythm pattern before conducting the whole orchestra.

10. Point to a group and have them start to chant their rhythm pattern in unison, and continue to chant it until you indicate that they must stop.

11. Then point to another group, who begin chanting their rhythm pattern along with the first group. This continues until all the groups are chanting at the same time.

Caveats and Options

1. Indicate increased and decreased speed as well as volume increase and reduction, with the appropriate hand gestures of an orchestra conductor.

2. Take groups in and out of the chant with an appropriate gesture.

3. At a suitable point, such as at the height of a crescendo or decrescendo, bring the piece to an end with a finalizing gesture.

4. The different groups can be asked to change their rhythm pattern. The sound patterns can also be whispered (loudly and stridently) if you wish to emphasize the consonants and consonant clusters.

5. Ask some of the students to conduct the orchestra.

6. If you have large classes, this can be a noisy activity. It is best done in a classroom where you are least likely to distract other classes.

7. Adult students will often get very involved in this activity if the teacher explains the rationale for doing it beforehand.

8. If the sound patterns listed above do not give practice in the particular sound production problems for the students in your class, invent other rhythmic patterns.

9. This activity is particularly useful with students from the same L1 background, as common problems in sound production can be focused on to the benefit of all the students.

Contributor

Dino Mahoney is Senior Lecturer in the English Department of the City Polytechnic of Hong Kong. The idea for the Sound and Rhythm Orchestra activity came out of a teaching collaboration with Erica Laine of the British Council, Hong Kong.

Minimal Pairs Triad

Levels
Any

Aims
Hear and pronounce
English phonemes

Class Time
1 minute/student

Preparation Time
5 minutes

Resources
Chalkboard, chalk
Minimal Pairs Handout
(see Appendix below)

The use of minimal pairs is probably the most frequently utilized exercise in pronunciation lessons: Students recite a list of paired words containing similar but distinct phonemes, and the teacher informs the students of their ability to contrast those sounds according to the phonemic system of the target language. Typically, this exercise is performed on a whole-class basis, with the speaker's ability known to every person in the room, while the other students sit idly awaiting a turn. By changing this exercise from a two-way task (speaker-teacher) into a three-way task (speaker-teacher-listeners), every member of the class can be engaged in the activity. Additionally, by the end of the lesson, all the students will have been apprised of their abilities without having the results publicized to the rest of the class.

Procedure

1. Write a list of minimal pairs emphasizing the target phonemes on the chalkboard.
2. Give each student a handout with lists of the same minimal pairs as are on the board. The list should appear on the handout as many times as there are students.
3. Have the first student circle at random one word from each pair on the handout.
4. While the first student pronounces the circled words, circle the words on the board that you hear.
5. Have the other students circle the words on their handouts that they think they hear.

   • Because the teacher is the assumed expert, the speaker has correctly pronounced the words if there is a match with the teacher's circled words on the board.

- Likewise, the listeners have correctly heard if the words they circled on their handouts under the column for Student 1 match the teacher's.
- For both the speaker and the listener, however, the correctness of the response is known only to the individual making the response.

6. Continue the process until all the students have had an opportunity to pronounce the words on the list.

Caveats and Options

1. If the L1 backgrounds of the students are varied, perform this activity on an individual basis because different language groups will have problems with different phonemes.
2. If the class has more than 20 students, spread the exercise out over a couple of periods to avoid boredom.
3. Have the students compare the number of words correctly pronounced before and after the lesson or for homework practice.

References and Further Reading

Nilsen, A. P. (1973). *Pronunciation contrasts*. New York: Regents.

Appendix: Sample Handout: /v/ and /b/

Student 1	Student 2	Student 3	Student 4
vote boat	vote boat	vote boat	vote boat
vow bow	vow bow	vow bow	vow bow
vet bet	vet bet	vet bet	vet bet
vest best	vest best	vest best	vest best

Contributor

Maura McCulloch is an associate faculty member in the Pima County Community College District in Tucson, Arizona, in the United States.

Vowel Symbols Through an Information Gap

Levels
Low intermediate +

Aims
Discover vowel symbols
(as used in systems of
broad transcription)
through a set of
communicative
procedures

Class Time
50 minutes

Preparation Time
30 minutes

Resources
Handouts (See
Appendices below)
Overhead projector
(OHP) and
transparencies

Students can benefit from focused practice with the sound system of English, but only if teachers are consistent in how such information is presented to them. Firth (1992) suggests the following:

> A pronunciation syllabus should begin with the widest possible focus and move gradually in on specific problems . . . [while relying on] a constantly shifting focus—from overall effectiveness of communication, to a specific problem, to overall effectiveness of communication, and so on. (p. 173)

Avery and Ehrlich (1992), Murphy (1991), and Morley (1991) agree that coherent instruction in oral communication needs to include attention to issues of communicative fluency as well as linguistic accuracy. One means for integrating such instruction in ESOL classrooms is to engage students in relatively more communicative activities even when they are being introduced to symbols used to represent the individual sound segments of the target language.

Procedure

I. Introducing Vowel Symbols

1. Present the Classroom Vowel Chart (see Appendix A) on a transparency to the class. These symbols and corresponding numbers represent the 14 primary vowel sounds in English as spoken in most sections of the United States and Canada.
2. Spend 2 or 3 minutes enunciating each of the individual vowel sounds in isolation.
3. Produce all of them in one continuous stream of speech by beginning with the high-front-tense vowel, /iy/, passing through the remaining set of front vowels, reaching the low-central /a/, continuing up

through the back vowels, passing through the high-back tense vowel, /uw/, and finishing with the schwa. (The first time you do this in one connected stream of speech, there is usually a spontaneous outburst of laughter from students in the class. Especially for L2 speakers of English, hearing all of the vowel sounds connected in a continuous stream of speech is a somewhat novel experience.)

4. Begin to demonstrate individual voice quality settings of the mouth, tongue, and jaw for each of these 14 vowel sounds. (Because you are building toward a relatively more communicative activity, these initial and rather traditional procedures for introducing the vowel sounds of English should continue for no more than 5–10 minutes.)

5. Begin to highlight the association of each of the 14 vowel sounds with their corresponding symbols and numbers as depicted in the chart.

6. Ask the students to call out a number from 1 to 14. Then enunciate the corresponding vowel sound in isolation.

7. Have the students call out a number. Then demonstrate the corresponding mouth and jaw setting silently, without actually producing the vowel sound. Have the students try to figure out which is the corresponding vowel number on the chart.

8. Have the students call out two numbers at a time. You then enunciate both of these vowel sounds, thus contrasting them (as in minimal pairs).

9. Have the students call out a number and you pronounce one of the following monosyllabic words corresponding with the student's selected number: *beat* (1), *bit* (2), *bait* (3), *bet* (4), *bat* (5), *bite* (6), *pot* (7), *bout* (8), *bought* (9), *boy* (10), *boat* (11), *put* (12), *boot* (13), and *but* (14). (In most standard dialects of North American English, these words can be used to contrast all of the 14 primary vowel sounds in a similar monosyllabic environment.)

10. Ask the students to call out a number from 1 to 14. You produce some other monosyllabic word/example that illustrates the targeted vowel sound.

11. Again, have the students call out two or more numbers and you pronounce the corresponding monosyllabic word or words.

Caveats and Options

1. Because this is an introductory lesson, there is only one midcentral vowel represented in the chart. Also, the chart uses a modified version of the Trager/Smith system of transcription, not the IPA system, because this is the most currently popular one in ESL texts available in the United States and Canada (e.g., Avery & Ehrlich, 1992; Handschuh & de Geigel, 1985; Orion, 1988; Prator & Robinette, 1985).
2. One reason for limiting the number of vowel sounds to 14 is to keep this initial lesson as accessible to students as possible. Symbols for the stressed midcentral and the stressed pre-/r/ midcentral vowels, for example, can be introduced in subsequent lessons.

II. The Information Gap Phase of the Lesson

1. After exploring the traditional procedures outlined above for 5–10 minutes, ask everyone to pair off.
2. Distribute one copy of the Primary Vowel Sounds Handout (see Appendix B) to one member of each pair. (On this sheet, the 14 primary vowel sounds discussed above are illustrated with five or six monosyllabic examples.)
3. In order to set up the information gap portion of the lesson, encourage the students to call out one of the words on the sheet and you indicate which is the corresponding vowel sound by either pointing to its location on the overhead or by simply saying its corresponding number aloud (e.g., Teacher: "Did you say *deep*? Oh, that would be vowel sound Number 1."). In this way, the students can begin to quiz the teacher on whether or not even a teacher is really able to distinguish between the sounds illustrated on the handout (an awareness raising activity).
4. While working in groups of two, one student has access to the Vowel Sounds Handout while the other student does not. At the same time, both students are able to see the information illustrated in the Vowel Chart because it is still being projected on a transparency at the front of the class. By following these procedures, there is a "knower" and a "learner" in each pair.

5. Ask the knower, who has access to all of the example monosyllabic words depicted in the handout, to select one word from the list and to say it clearly to the partner.

6. Then, ask the learner to try to identify which of the 14 vowel symbols corresponds with the word selected by the knower. The learner can accomplish this by identifying the appropriate number depicted on the chart on the transparency.

7. Periodically ask students to switch roles and take turns acting as a knower and a learner.

8. While pairs of students are working with the sound system material, consult with individual groups, provide additional examples, model accurate pronunciations of the individual words, suggest additional instructional strategies to the knower, encourage the learners, and so forth.

9. By the end of a 1-hour class, the students will have had many practice opportunities for working with and beginning to recognize the 14 primary vowel sounds of English.

Caveats and Options

1. The reason for involving students in these procedures is to engage them in an information gap activity that provides opportunities for a significant degree of peer interaction and collaboration.

2. Because this is partly a guessing game activity, the knower has the option of making the exchange a little easier for the partner by indicating, for example, that the target sound is one of the numbers from 1 to 5 (a front vowel), or one of the numbers from 9 to 13 (a back vowel), or one of the central vowels (Numbers 6, 7, 8, or 14), and so forth.

3. The knower could take steps to limit the learner's choices even further by pointing to an even smaller set of symbols or by orally listing a set of three or four numbers from which the learner could select.

4. Of course, at some point you might want to model these instructional strategies for the whole class, but eventually students are encouraged to begin managing the knower role on their own with less teacher intervention.

5. Eventually, you can build upon these initial information gap procedures by:

- introducing parallel lessons that are focused upon consonant sounds and symbols
- selecting a course text that uses the same or similar set of symbols to represent English sounds
- making reference to sound-symbol information whenever students have questions about how particular words should be pronounced
- building upon these introductory lessons in order to highlight suprasegmental aspects of the sound system such as stress, rhythm, and intonation
- pointing out the high frequency nature of the unstressed midcentral vowel in English
- creating a classroom wall chart that depicts vowel symbols in a grid located at the center of the chart, and symbols for the 24 primary consonant symbols arranged from top to bottom with 12 symbols on the left-hand side and 12 symbols on the right-hand side (see Appendix C)
- spending class time on related activities that are based upon the students developing a recognition ability with samples of broad transcription
- being consistent in drawing the students' attentions to sound-spelling relationships.

6. You might also want to move beyond monosyllabic examples and begin to work with the identification of vowel sounds in polysyllabic words and phrases.

7. You can spend time highlighting the role of overall fluency and general speaking habits such as expressiveness, speed, loudness, and clarity of speech along with giving focused attention to sound segments.

8. You can use some alternative set of symbols that is based upon the IPA, dictionary symbols, or some other system of transcription (if one of these would be more useful to students).

9. Spend time highlighting the importance of suprasegmentals (stress, rhythm, intonation) and introduce more than the 14 primary vowel

sounds discussed above. These might include symbols for the stressed mid-central vowel, the stressed mid-central pre-/r/ vowel, the unstressed mid-central pre-/r/ vowel, and other vowel sounds.

References and Further Reading

Avery, P., & Ehrlich, S. (Eds.). (1992). *Teaching American English pronunciation* (pp. 221–227). New York: Oxford University Press.

Firth, S. (1992). Pronunciation syllabus design: A question of focus. In P. Avery & S. Ehrlich (Eds.), *Teaching American English pronunciation* (pp. 173–183). New York: Oxford University Press.

Handschuh, J., & de Geigel, A. (1985). *Improving oral communication: A pronunciation oral-communication manual*. Englewood Cliffs, NJ: Prentice Hall.

Morley, J. (1991). The pronunciation component in teaching English to speakers of other languages. *TESOL Quarterly*, *25*, 481–520.

Murphy, J. (1991). Oral communication in TESOL: Integrating speaking, listening and pronunciation. *TESOL Quarterly*, *25*, 51–75.

Orion, G. F. (1988). *Pronouncing American English: Sounds, stress, and intonation*. New York: Newbury House.

Prator, C., & Robinette, B. (1985). *Manual of American English pronunciation* (4th ed.). New York: Holt, Rinehart & Winston.

Appendix A: Classroom Vowel Chart: Symbols for 14 Primary Vowel Sounds

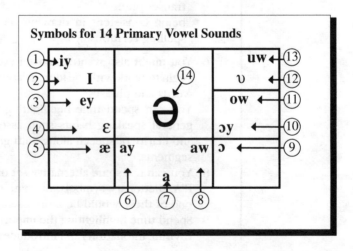

Symbols for 14 Primary Vowel Sounds

Appendix B: Examples of the 14 Primary Vowel Sounds in Monosyllabic Words

1. /iy/	2. /ɪ/	3. /ey/	4. /ɛ/
deep	hit	rain	said
weak	tick	gate	bet
he's	did	base	rest
beach	his	pain	them
freeze	rich	Jane	get
greed	lift	play	left
team	hid	tape	head

5. /æ/	6. /ay/	7. /a/	8. /aw/
pass	like	sock	pound
shack	lied	clock	town
grass	high	stop	now
back	life	hot	found
catch	my	got	out
bag	bride	shock	brown
grad	side	jog	doubt

9. /ɔ/	10. /y/	11. /ow/	12. /ʊ/
ought	boy	float	took
thought	toy	slow	good
tall	Roy	vote	could
off	poise	close	stood
walk	joy	rope	wood
hall	point	grow	look
jaw	noise	coat	should
dawn	Floyd	load	cook

13. /uw/	14. /ə/
soup	luck
hoop	blood
new	cup
two	was
who	tuck
stew	come
shoe	mud
Luke	none

Appendix C: Classroom Wall Chart: Vowel and Consonant Symbols*

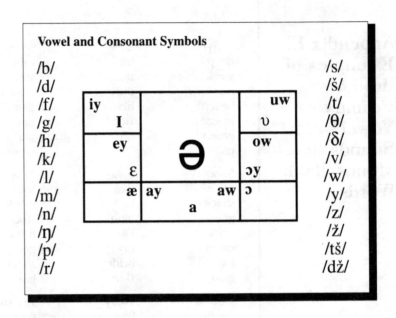

Vowel and Consonant Symbols

/b/
/d/
/f/
/g/
/h/
/k/
/l/
/m/
/n/
/ŋ/
/p/
/r/

/s/
/š/
/t/
/θ/
/ð/
/v/
/w/
/y/
/z/
/ž/
/tš/
/dž/

*(Modified Trager-Smith)

Contributor

John M. Murphy is Associate Professor of Applied Linguistics and ESL at Georgia State University. His publications have appeared in TESOL Journal, TESOL Quarterly, English for Specific Purposes, TESL Canada Journal, *and other L2 journals.*

Minimal Pair Identification Drills

Levels
Any

Aims
Learn English
pronunciation contrasts

Class Time
10–15 minutes

Preparation Time
1 hour

Resources
Handouts (see
Appendix below)
Pronunciation guide of
minimal pairs

Numerous pronunciation texts for ESL students (e.g., Orion, 1988) provide learners with practice in identifying and producing vowel and consonant sounds. However, few activities allow for both skills to occur simultaneously with feedback coming only from classmates. The following activity fulfills a need for this type of pronunciation activity.

Procedure

1. Pair off students and give one of each handout to each pair of students.
2. Have students first say the number of the item and then only the word underlined on their particular handout for that item.
3. Have partners check off the word they hear and pronounce their underlined word for that item.
4. Depending upon the level of the students, request that they not repeat each underlined word more than twice.
5. Tell the students not to look at each other's handouts nor in any way (besides pronouncing) to indicate to their partner which underlined word is being produced.

Caveats and Options

1. Students may accomplish this activity working with a single partner or may even change partners after each item, but they must be careful to write down the name of each partner for a particular item.
2. Ask the students to correct each other's handouts and discover their pronunciation errors.
3. Emphasize that it is not necessarily the speaker nor the listener who is in error, but possibly a combination of both.
4. Tell the students to sign their papers and collect them for future reference.

References and Further Reading

Appendix: Preparing the Handout

5. This activity can be adapted to any ability level as well as to a specific L1 depending upon the learners' pronunciation problems.

Henrichsen, L. (1978). Peer-tutoring pronunciation contrasts. *English Teaching Forum, 16*, 18.

Orion, G. (1988). *Pronouncing American English*. New York: Newbury House.

1. Prepare two sets of handouts with the same sets of words. Each set should require the opposite word in the pair to be targeted for pronunciation and comprehension.

   - For example, given a choice of two words (e.g., *pan* and *dan*), Student A should be required to pronounce *pan* while Student B should be asked to pronounce *dan*.
   - Have students pronounce only those words underlined on their own copy of the handout. (See examples, such as those in italics below.)

2. Create several variations of the handout by underlining different words on three or four copies of the original word list.
3. Save these variations as master copies for future lessons.
4. The original word list should be created with the pronunciation problems of the students in mind.

   - Include in the handout several examples of the same contrasting sounds in various minimal word pairs.
   - Use several sounds to discover individual pronunciation difficulties.

5. Ask students to pronounce the words in italics below one at a time and then check off those said by their partner.

Minimal pair contrast with consonant sounds

a.	[　] *west*	[　] vest	
b.	[　] year	[　] *jeer*	
c.	[　] rock	[　] *lock*	
d.	[　] *pie*	[　] buy	

Minimal pair contrast with vowel sounds

e. [   ] set   [   ] *sit*
f. [   ] *met*   [   ] mat
g. [   ] *far*   [   ] fur
h. [   ] *shut*   [   ] shot

6. Include items in the handout that distribute the same sounds but in different positions. For example, the sounds /f/ with /v/ and the sounds /p/ with /b/ are contrasted in various letter positions below.

Initial position

i. [   ] fast   [   ] *vast*
j. [   ] pest   [   ] *best*

Middle position

k. [   ] *refuse*   [   ] reviews
l. [   ] staple   [   ] *stable*

Final position

m. [   ] *safe*   [   ] save
n. [   ] *rip*   [   ] rib

7. Include at the end of the handout word choices in sets of three. For example:

o. [   ] cat   [   ] *cut*   [   ] cot
p. [   ] sip   [   ] ship   [   ] *zip*
q. [   ] *bass*   [   ] bash   [   ] bath
r. [   ] *tall*   [   ] toil   [   ] tool
s. [   ] ball   [   ] *boil*   [   ] bull

Contributor

Phil Plourde is a faculty member of the Center for English as a Second Language at the University of Southern Illinois, in the United States.

The Memory Game

Levels
Any

Aims
Listen to, focus on, and
recite long lists of
words with the same
phonemes and have fun
while doing it

Class Time
5–10 minutes

Preparation Time
None

Resources
None

Students do not receive enough practice in forming sounds and pronouncing words by repeating them once, twice, or even three times. A great deal of practice is needed, but it can become tedious, with students tuning out instead of in. Motivation is inherent in this activity because it is a game. In the memory game, the students use the vocabulary they already know to practice sounds they need to acquire for pronunciation improvement. They also have the opportunity to practice vocabulary that their classmates already know. Repetition and practice comes not from listening to their teacher but from listening to each other.

Procedure

1. Tell the students which sound they are going to practice, and give some examples of words which start with that sound. (Your examples cannot be used during the game.)
2. Start the game by giving the first word. The game should be started with a more proficient student, but continue in order, either around the room or up and down the rows.
3. The first student repeats the word the teacher offered, and then adds a new word that begins with the same sound. (One actual chain from a class went like this: *chocolate, chalk, champion, chop, church, chair, check, change, choose, chosen, charcoal.*)
4. As the game continues, students who cannot recite and/or add are out. (However, you should be very patient with these students and give them time to answer.)

Caveats and Options

1. This activity is a great way to begin or end a class, or to reinforce sounds the class is practicing. It also lets you know what vocabulary the students have acquired.

2. Sometimes when students are eliminated from a game, they lose interest and become disruptive. A way to prevent this is to assign a point to the student who has been unable to respond, giving him/her the chance to respond the next time. The student(s) who have the fewest points win.
3. Another option is to have a game without winners. In this way, you may prompt students when they cannot remember a word, allowing the respondent to continue.

Contributor

Caryn Schlesinger teaches ESL to elementary school, middle school, and high school students at the North Shore School District in Glen Head, New York in the United States.

Tongue Twisters

Levels
Beginning–intermediate

Aims
Practice pronouncing
specific English sound
segments

Class Time
15–30

Preparation Time
15 minutes

Resources
Chalkboard and chalk
Short tongue twisters
typed on strips of paper
(see Appendix below)

Tongue Twister is a popular game enjoyed by children and adults alike. This activity aims at consolidating the English sounds students have learned by creating a gamelike atmosphere for practice. It is wise to include tongue twisters that highlight particularly problematic minimal sound differences for your class (e.g., pronunciation of /f/ and /v/; /s/ and /š/; /f/ and /θ/).

Procedure

1. Explain the task to the students.
2. Introduce the sounds students are to practice and write their symbols on the board.
3. Ask students to suggest words that illustrate the various sounds written on the board.
4. Read aloud the words and ask students to listen carefully.
5. Read aloud words, randomly selected from the list, and ask students to identify the words by watching the movement of your mouth and tongue.
6. Have the students try to produce the sounds.
7. Divide the class into groups and have each group sitting or standing in single file.
8. Distribute a short, typed tongue twister to the first student in each group and ask him/her to learn it by heart.
9. Take away the strips of paper.
10. Have each student repeat the tongue twister to the next person in line. That person repeats the message to the next in line. In this way, the message is passed from one student to the next.
11. Have the last student to hear the tongue twister in each group write it on the board.

12. The group finishing correctly in the shortest time wins the game.
13. Repeat the process with another tongue twister.

Caveats and Options

1. You and students should decide on a clear set of rules in advance. For example, how many times can each group member repeat the tongue twister to one another? Does spelling count in the dictation session?
2. An alternative way to report back is to have the last student in each group say the tongue twister out loud. If the class size is small, you can organize an in-class competition to select the fastest speaker.
3. Students enjoy this activity very much and demonstrate great enthusiasm in producing the sounds as well as in spelling words correctly to win the game. This exercise should be done fairly briskly and should proceed from slow to fast to add challenge.
4. This game is also suitable for higher level students by adjusting the level of difficulty of the tongue twisters.

Appendix: Sample Tongue Twisters

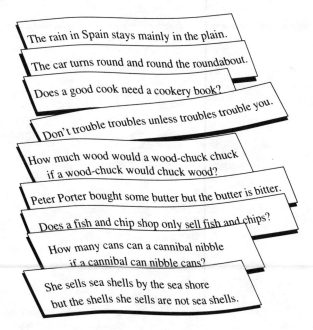

The rain in Spain stays mainly in the plain.

The car turns round and round the roundabout.

Does a good cook need a cookery book?

Don't trouble troubles unless troubles trouble you.

How much wood would a wood-chuck chuck if a wood-chuck would chuck wood?

Peter Porter bought some butter but the butter is bitter.

Does a fish and chip shop only sell fish and chips?

How many cans can a cannibal nibble if a cannibal can nibble cans?

She sells sea shells by the sea shore but the shells she sells are not sea shells.

Contributor

Pauline Tam is Assistant Lecturer at the City Polytechnic of Hong Kong, where she teaches reading, writing, and business communication. She has also taught EFL for many years in Hong Kong secondary schools.

Sounds Before Visual Clues

Levels
Any

Aims
Recognize IPA
(International Phonetic
Alphabet)
Develop ability to
pronounce new words
correctly according to
IPA transcription

Class Time
30–40 minutes

Preparation Time
Variable

Resources
Cards with pictures of
objects or animals

This technique is best used to introduce the International Phonetic Alphabet (IPA) for beginning adult students. Most students have dictionaries with the IPA as the pronunciation guide, but many of them have not been taught how to pronounce the IPA symbols. The pronunciation of new words is usually introduced in company with the spelling of the words, which tends to trigger the phoneme-grapheme correspondence of the students' L1, thus creating the potential for interference. With this technique, the learner may minimize the potential interference from the phoneme-grapheme correspondence and from the very beginning may understand that the pronunciation of English words in many cases does not correspond with the spelling of the words. This activity tries to ensure accurate pronunciation at the early stages of language learning and minimize the influence of the L1 while building students' confidence to work independently.

Procedure

1. Present a picture card to students and name the object in the picture several times. If the name of the object is written on the card, make sure at this point that the students do not see the spelling of the word.
2. Ask students to repeat after you until they pronounce the intended sound in the name correctly.
3. Present the students with another picture card designed to elicit the same sound and repeat Steps 1 and 2 until all the picture cards for the same sound have been presented.
4. Present a new set of picture cards for a new sound and repeat Steps 1, 2, and 3.

5. Present a picture card to students. This time, show students only the IPA symbols for English sounds. (The students still do not see the whole word.)
6. Read aloud only the sound of the IPA symbol, not the whole word, several times. Then ask students to repeat the sound in isolation until you are satisfied with their pronunciation.
7. Present a new card for the same sound and repeat Step 6 as often as needed.
8. Present a new set of picture cards for a new sound and repeat Steps 5, 6, and 7.

Caveats and Options

1. For the picture cards, choose pictures of objects or animals whose names contain the vowel and consonant sounds you want to introduce.
2. Create several picture cards for each sound by drawing pictures or clipping them from magazines or newspapers and then pasting them onto cards.
3. Don't show the students how the words are spelled. Have them concentrate instead on how the words are pronounced. Visual spelling clues may lead students to pronounce new words using the phoneme-grapheme correspondence of their L1, thus creating interference. This is especially the case when students hear an English sound that either does not exist or is very close to some of the sounds in their L1.
4. This technique is for pronunciation improvement rather than for communicative skills development. It is best used during the early period of a pronunciation course. When learners have satisfactorily demonstrated their pronunciation, the classroom activities should be made more communicative and contextualized.
5. Pairwork and groupwork are possible for such exercises as:

   - Pair Dictations: Student A and Student B give one another dictations at the single-sound level or the sentence level as you decide.
   - Team Effort: For intermediate learners and above, a group of four or five members provide words with the sound or sound clusters. They can then practice them within a limited time.

- Group Competition: See which group provides more words with the intended sound(s) within a limited time.

6. Students' progress may be assessed through oral tests that, for example, ask students to read sentences or short passages transcribed in IPA symbols or give oral presentations.

Contributor

Yongmin Zhu is an ESL instructor at Los Medanos College in Pittsburgh, California in the United States and has an MA in Linguistics/TESOL from the University of Utah.

♦ Suprasegmental Phonemes
Stress Stretch

Level
Any

Aims
Gain awareness of
stressed syllables
Associate stress with
vowel length, clarity,
and pitch
Internalize these
concepts into body
memory
Pronounce polysyllabic
words with proper
stress and intonation

Class Time
15 minutes

Preparation Time
15 minutes

Resources
Chalkboard or other
writing surface

Some learners have difficulty perceiving the difference between stressed and unstressed syllables in English. If their perception is weak, they also have difficulty producing the rhythm of words and phrases with correct stress and intonation. The Stress Stretch integrates kinesthetic, tactile, visual, and auditory perception to aid in the production of proper stress. I developed the stress stretch to complement and amplify other techniques for indicating stressed syllables to learners of English. Although I have used it with learners of all language proficiencies, it is particularly beneficial for the fluent speaker whose stress and rhythm patterns are fossilized and in need of a dramatic push toward change.

Procedure

1. Prepare a list of polysyllabic words within the learners' vocabulary range. Include words of two, three, four, and five syllables, as appropriate. For example:

   apple　　banana　　avocado　　strawberry　　cauliflower

2. Mark the word to indicate the stressed syllable. For example:

   ápple　　banána　　avocádo　　stráwberry　　cáuliflower
   or
   APple　　baNANa　　avoCAdo　　STRAWberry　　CAUliflower

3. Explain that a stressed syllable is longer, clearer, stronger and often higher in pitch than an unstressed syllable.

4. Pronounce each word on the list, exaggerating the stressed syllable slightly.

5. Sit on a chair. Model the stress stretch. Pronounce each word again, this time rising to a full standing position on the stressed syllable

252

and returning to a sitting position on the unstressed syllables in a synchronic fashion.

6. Have students (freed of books, pens, or other encumbrances) pronounce each word, rising to a standing position on the stressed syllable and returning to a sitting position on the unstressed syllables. Let them do the stress stretch first with you and then without your lead.

Caveats and Options

1. During subsequent lessons, when students encounter difficulty pronouncing polysyllabic words with proper stress, have them do a stress stretch as they pronounce the target words.
2. As students do the stress stretch, have them observe each other. Remind them to synchronize their upward and downward motions with their vocalized stress pattern of each word. For example, they should avoid stretching their bodies but not their vowels in stressed syllables.
3. Have more advanced speakers perform the stress stretch with phrases and sentences in paragraphs.
4. As an option, have students open their eyes wide on each stressed syllable.
5. If students don't have chairs, have them rise from a crouching position.

References and Further Reading

Chan, M. (1987). *Using your hands to teach pronunciation*. This videotape for teacher educators has been demonstrated to teachers at several TESOL conventions, at state conferences, and at teacher preparation workshops. It also demonstrates other pronunciation teaching techniques and is available from the author.

Contributor

Marsha Chan teaches ESL at Mission College in Santa Clara, California in the United States. She has published a book and videotapes on pronunciation and authored articles on oral communication.

Practice With Tag Questions

Levels
Beginning–intermediate

Aims
Practice producing tag
questions

Class Time
Varies

Preparation Time
30 minutes

Resources
Note cards
Audiotaped dialogue

In this activity, students use rising and falling intonation to communicate purposefully. (The different intonation patterns associated with tag questions indicate the speaker's degree of sureness about the topic.) Feedback on accuracy is given by the peers, not the teacher. Students respond enthusiastically to this activity and are attentive to matching the appropriate intonation with the speaker's purpose.

Procedure

1. Prepare students for the activity by explaining the use of rising and falling intonation in tag questions. Give examples.
2. Have them listen to a dialogue in which two speakers are using rising and falling intonation alternately to ask a question and seek agreement. (Prepare the tape in such a way that following the dialogue, the speakers on the tape say the tag questions and allow time for the students to decide if the speaker was unsure [question] or sure [seeking agreement] of the content of the question.)
3. Give each student three notecards. On one notecard write the word *sure*. On the second notecard, write the word *unsure*. On the third notecard write four or five questions and after each question, print either *sure* or *unsure*.
4. Tell students to read each question aloud using the appropriate intonation to ask a question or seek agreement.
5. Have the rest of the students listen to the speaker and hold up either their "sure" or "unsure" card according to what they heard the speaker say. (The speaker is able to check the accuracy of his or

her intended speech production but is not necessarily required to share it with the class.)

6. Have the next student read his/her first question.

Contributor

Gina Crocetti is completing her MA in TESOL at Portland State University (PSU). She teaches speaking/listening at PSU as well as reading/writing and preliteracy in a program she designed for St. Vincent Hospital.

Sentence Intonation Fluency

Levels
Beginning–intermediate

Aims
Develop sentence-level
pronunciation and
intonation
Deliver appropriate
sentences that express
feelings

Class Time
Variable

Preparation Time
1 hour

Resources
Sentence Worksheet
Classroom with seating
for group work

In this activity, you set the tasks in which learners have the opportunity to use short sentences in meaningful contexts. Learners can develop an awareness of the role of emphasis through tone, pitch, volume, and framing. The activity provides fluency practice and pronunciation development with peers and develops an awareness of the role of situation by using the learners' L1 knowledge of social situations to link meaning and spoken delivery. In the sentence-based tasks, the learners speak in pairs then use greater expression, followed by a simple procedure to create situations to practice other vocabulary.

Procedure

1. Create a worksheet of sentence groupings each of which contain similar sentences of increasing length and complexity (e.g., *I'd choose blue. I'd choose blue shoes. I'd choose blue shoes to take to school. I'd rather choose blue shoes to take to school to use. I'd rather choose blue shoes to take to school to use if I were you*).
2. Discuss and give students examples of framing (the use of space), emphasis (weight on words), and tone.
3. Brainstorm adjectives of expression and link them with examples of oral delivery (e.g., draw attention to the role of feeling and emphasis on key words to show how emphasis on one word can convey a range of meanings through varied delivery, for example, *I really love you*).
4. Group the class in mixed ability groupings of four and have students pair off in the group.
5. Give each pair of students a sentence group and have them talk with their partner, reading the sentences which are of increasing length.

6. Taking turns, have one student in each pair speak the sentences to the other pair, thinking of an emotion that they wish to convey. The pair who has been listening guesses the key word(s) and the feeling expressed while concentrating on the use of stress and space between words.

7. Have the pair who has been listening choose two of the sentences and script a preceding and following sentence that would match the intonation pattern chosen by the speaker. (In modeling this step, the teacher can highlight how intonation relates to situation, setting, and purpose.)

8. Have the pairs swap roles.

Caveats and Options

1. The activity needs clear step-by-step instructions. It is highly guided in form in that the sentences are written on the worksheet but has potential for freer oral production in the scripting procedure.

2. A class round robin of different examples can provide opportunities for fluency practice.

3. Pronunciation practice can serve as a jumping off point for script writing based on a favorite expressive sentence.

Contributor

Stephen Hall has taught, done research, and conducted ESOL teacher preparation seminars in New Zealand, the Western Pacific, and in Southeast Asia. Focusing on talk and content learning as well as interaction in the classroom, he has written classroom and teacher training materials and a range of specialized oral skills courses.

Word-Set Improvisations

Levels
High beginning–
intermediate

Aims
Increase intonational
variation
Highlight stress and
rhythm in conversation
to sound more
expressive

Class Time
10–20 minutes

Preparation Time
10–20 minutes

Resources
Situation cards

In this activity, students improvise situations, but instead of trying to use language that may be beyond their capabilities, they use lexical items from word sets, for example, numbers, names, and letters of the alphabet. In this way they practice topically related turn taking without having to structure entire sentences, questions, or imperatives.

Procedure

1. Pair off students or group them in threes or fours.
2. Give each group a different situation card and ask the students to think about how they could improvise a short scene around that situation. The situation cards might include the following:

   - You want to go to the cinema. You try and persuade two of your friends to go with you.
   - You have lent a friend some money, and she hasn't paid you back. You go to her house, and in front of her family, you ask for your money back.
   - You are a bit late for an appointment. When you arrive, your friends have already left. You are very upset. You meet them the next day.
   - You are playing cards with some people. You think one of them is cheating.

3. Monitor the students' work, helping the different groups with ideas.
4. Ask each group to improvise their situation. However, instead of asking the students to use language that may be beyond their capabilities, ask them to use a particular word set (e.g., letters of the alphabet, numbers, colors, names). For example, if the improvisation situation is one in which students suspect others of cheating, they could use lexical items from the color set:

A: (Accusing tone) Yellow, green, purple
B: (Defensive) Red
A: (Angry) Yellow
B: (Defensive) Green, blue, brown, grey
A: (Very annoyed) Yellow . . . blue, green, black

In this example, the use of colors is completely arbitrary. What matters is the students' intonation. As another example, in the case where one person owes the other money, lexical items from the numbers set could be used to negotiate repayment:

A: Twenty dollars!
B: No! Ten dollars!
A: Twenty dollars—on the fourteenth!
B: No! Ten dollars on the eighteenth!
A: Two o'clock!
B: No. Five o'clock.

5. Have the groups practice their improvisations.
6. Then have them act out the situations in front of the class. Have the audience try to understand what is happening by interpreting the language and the paralinguistic features of the improvisations.
7. Question the class after each improvisation to make sure they have understood. Your questions can lead the audience to expand on these skeletal utterances. For instance, in the example above, Student A's comment "Twenty dollars!" means "You owe me twenty dollars."

Caveats and Options

1. For intermediate students, these improvisations can act as the groundwork for further improvisations around the same situation, using more developed natural speech, instead of lexical items from word sets. This will then give a chance for the expressiveness explored in the word-set improvisation to be transferred into normal spoken interactions.
2. For lower level students, their L1 may be used in the preparation stage of the improvisation.
3. For more advanced students, issues of register can be introduced (e.g., formality/informality, relative power and solidarity of the speakers).

4. It is important that the rationale for this activity be made clear to the students.

Contributor

Dino Mahoney is Senior Lecturer in the English Department of the City Polytechnic of Hong Kong.

Pronunciation Project

Levels
Any

Aims
Listen to enjoyable music
Transcribe song lyrics and share them

Class Time
Variable

Preparation Time
1–2 hours

Resources
Audiotape player

Popular music is an exciting departure from old fashioned dialogues when it comes to practicing pronunciation and merely getting students used to speaking English. Partaking in this project allows students to practice their English and to involve their classmates in what they are doing and what they are interested in. The motivation level is high and the results can be amazing.

Procedure

1. Play a song for the class that coincides with the unit the class is studying. For instance, if the students are studying Valentine's Day, "Cupid" (sung by Sam Cooke), "That's What Friends Are For" (sung by Dionne Warwick), or any love song may be presented.
2. Have the students first listen to the song to see if they can guess what the title is or what the song is about.
3. Write (or have a student help you write) these ideas on the board.
4. Next, distribute copies of the lyrics of the song.
5. Have the students listen to the song as they read the words.
6. Discuss the song and check students' predictions.
7. Then have students engage in a line-by-line oral repetition of the song. (By this time, they are usually quite ready to sing.)
8. Use the song as an oral warm-up for as long as the unit is being studied.
9. Give students an assignment to find songs that match the theme being studied. Have students pick a song with English lyrics and transcribe the words. (Also have students record the song on audiotape if it isn't in that form already.)

10. Have students write a summary of the song, telling what the song is about, who wrote it, who performs it, why they like it, and anything else significant about it.

11. The students must make enough copies of the lyrics for the whole class for their oral presentations, when students talk about the song and the information they used in their summary.

12. At the end of each presentation, have students distribute the lyrics so everyone can sing the song.

Caveats and Options

1. One full period is usually required for the introduction of the project. Then time must be made for students to present their own projects. Three or four students can present during a 40–minute class period.

2. No preparation is required for those periods when students present their projects.

3. This is an effective pronunciation and listening task because in order to transcribe, the student must listen to the song over and over again. Students are very careful about transcribing because their friends will notice their mistakes when they listen to and read the lyrics.

4. It may be wise for the teacher to have the students sign up for a song they want to present and give a copy to the teacher. This will prevent two problems: two or more students presenting the same song and the use of songs with inappropriate language. The teacher should explain to the class that songs with inappropriate language may not be presented.

Contributor

Caryn Schlesinger teaches ESL to elementary school, middle school, and high school students at the North Shore School District in Glen Head, New York, in the United States.

Part IV: Speaking in Specific Contexts

◆ Oral Presentations Speakers and Listeners as Partners

Levels
Intermediate +

Aims
Practice speaking, listening, note-taking, and evaluating

Class Time
Variable over a 3-week period

Preparation Time
Several class hours

Resources
Outline form (see Appendix A below)
Speaker evaluation forms (see Appendices B–C below)

Oral presentations often provide practice in speaking for the presenter but do not develop the listening skills of the audience. This activity helps speakers and listeners become productive partners in the ESOL classroom.

Procedure

1. Have students build oral presentations around a common topic so that each participant can contribute equally. In this activity, the topic is the countries represented in the class.
2. Have the students discuss what they would like to learn about their classmates' countries and create a composite outline. (Type this for them after class, leaving space between sections for note-taking.)
3. Allow students to report on any country except their own and to work in pairs provided that the partners have different L1s. For example, a student from Taiwan and one from Korea might work together on a presentation about Thailand. The student from Thailand serves as a resource person for that team, helping to verify information gathered from sources in the library.
4. Make sure each team member decides which part of the outline to cover and organizes the information on note cards (to use while speaking).
5. Discuss presentation techniques with the students and encourage them to practice.
6. During each presentation, ask those not presenting to take notes on the outline forms. (See Appendix A below.) Collect and evaluate these forms.

7. Following each presentation, have each listener fill out a speaker evaluation form. (See Appendix B below.) Variables such as preparation, smooth transitions, and appropriate use of movement can be judged on a scale of 1–5.
8. These forms are collected by another student in the room and are given to the student presenter.
9. When all presentations have been completed, give each student a written evaluation of his preparation, presentation and note-taking participation. (See Appendix C below.)

Caveats and Options

1. Students can use this method to develop presentations on their fields of interest, or at a lower level, on how to make or do something.
2. Oral presentations on different countries require a diverse group. When only one or a few countries are represented, look for other topics that will allow cooperative participation.

Appendix A: Sample Outline for Oral Presentations

Country Name

I.   Location

II. Geography
     A. Topography
     B. Climate
     C. People

III. Language

IV. Population

V.   Economy
     A. Agriculture
     B. Industry
     C. Trade
     D. Government
     E. Currency

VI. History

VII. Education
   A. Elementary
   B. High School
   C. College

VIII. Religion

IX. Culture
   A. Traditions
   B. Local Customs
   C. National Dress
   D. Food
   E. Music
   F. Festivals
   G. Holidays
   H. Sports

X. Famous Places
   A. Important Cities
   B. Tourist Attractions

Appendix B: Sample Evaluation Form (for students)

Presenter(s): _____ _____ _____

Name of Country: _____

Directions: Quickly answer the following questions about the presentation after the presenters have finished. Circle the number you think best applies to the speaker. Number 5 is the highest score. Number 1 is the lowest. Write any comments on the lines below.

1. Did the speaker(s) deliver the presentation clearly and confidently?

   5   4   3   2   1

   _____

2. Did the speaker(s) seem well prepared?

   5   4   3   2   1

   _____

3. Did the speaker(s) move smoothly from idea to idea?

   5   4   3   2   1

_____

4. Did the speaker(s) use adequate examples and explanations?

   5   4   3   2   1

_____

5. Did the speaker(s) use movement and gestures appropriately?

   5   4   3   2   1

_____

6. Did the speaker(s) make eye contact with the listeners?

   5   4   3   2   1

_____

7. Did the speaker(s) make good use of supplemental materials?

   5   4   3   2   1

_____

Appendix C: Sample Evaluation Form (for teacher)

Name: _____ Level: _____

Preparation

Note cards: Correct form _____ organization _____ clarity _____

Bibliography: Correct form _____

Supplementary materials: _____

G = good   F = fair   P = poor

                                              Grade _____

Presentation

Strengths: _____

_____

_____

Suggestions: _____

_____

_____

Grade _____

Note-taking Participation

Total number of presentations _____

Completed sets of notes _____

Comments: _____

_____

_____

Contributor

Linda S. Abe teaches ESL in the Intensive English Program at Indiana University in the United States. When teaching in Japan, she authored three listening and speaking textbooks.

Weekend Stories

This activity is designed to encourage students to share their own experiences in English. With lower level students, stories are most successful when the students work within a specific linguistic framework. In this activity, the teacher whispers any needed corrections to the speaker and gets that person to repeat the correct version out loud.

Procedure

1. Introduce a pattern similar to the one below:
   Hello everybody. My name is _____. I have a story for you. On (Saturday/Sunday) I went (to) _____. I liked it because _____. Do you have any questions for me?
2. Have a student use this frame to describe the previous weekend.
3. Have the class respond with three or four standard questions that can be asked for any story that follows the pattern. For example:

   a. Did you have fun?
   b. Did you speak English?
   c. Who did you go with?
   d. When did you go?

4. During this activity, stand next to the student who is speaking. If the weekend storyteller or the student asking the question is having difficulties, whisper the correct phrase to the student and have him or her repeat it.
5. You may also correct by rephrasing the statement or question aloud for the entire class. Do not interrupt students for correction until they have completed the entire phrase.

6. If the class is unable to generate any questions for the speaker, move around the class and whisper one of the standard questions to a student.
7. Have that student ask the question of the speaker. In order to ensure success, be prepared to move from the speaker to the questioner and back to the speaker.
8. As the class begins to master the weekend story pattern, expand the story and the questioning by whispering additional phrases or questions to the students.

Caveats and Options

1. Decide carefully which errors to respond to and which to ignore.
2. As the students improve, you won't need to employ the whispering technique as often and can ask the students to tell their weekend stories in small groups.
3. Ask each group to pick one or two weekend stories that they think the whole class would enjoy.
4. Share your own weekend story with the class. Ask comprehension questions.
5. If more reticent students do not volunteer to tell their weekend stories, develop their confidence: Have them use this pattern to respond initially:

> Hello. My name is _____. Do you have any questions for me?

Contributors

Peter Hastorf specializes in oral language development. He enjoys creating activities that enliven his classes at the Taipei American School in Taiwan. Arlene Orensky is currently teaching at Taipei American School in Taiwan. She has presented workshops and coauthored two books for teachers in Asia.

Lecture Reports

Levels
Advanced

Aims
Develop formal
presentation skills
(rehearsed language)
Develop audience
interaction skills
(unrehearsed language)
Develop awareness of
effective presentation
styles from observing
public talks and lectures

Class Time
20 minutes/student

Preparation Time
30 minutes

Resources
Chalkboard and chalk
or overhead projector
(OHP) and markers

Students are often asked to give presentations on topics for which they will have to do the research. One way to decrease the complexity of such a task is to have them report on a lecture given outside class. Such an activity also enables ESOL students to observe live speakers at work and evaluate their effectiveness. A follow-up question and answer period with classmates allows students to develop confidence in their ability to interact with an audience without a prepared text.

Procedure

1. Gather information on upcoming lectures and public presentations in your area and pass out the schedule and topics of the lectures to the class early in the semester.
2. Have students choose and attend a lecture of interest to them and prepare a presentation for the class on the lecture content. (Students should observe the speaker's style and comment on the general over-all effectiveness of the speaker.)
3. Prepare the students before the lectures by discussing criteria for effective public speaking. (Modeling some effective techniques may help students become more aware of the strengths and weaknesses of a speaker during the lecture.)
4. Have students schedule presentations to their class within 2 weeks of the lecture they attended.
5. The format should keep students on a strict time frame (e.g., 10 minutes for formal report and 10 minutes for a question-and-answer period). Students should be reminded that they should summarize the lecture and avoid rambling.
6. During the question and answer period, have classmates ask present-ers for additional information or for their thoughts on various aspects

of the lecture topic. (This step can provide students in the audience with confidence in speaking out in large group settings.)

7. Have presenters prepare for possible questions from the audience. They should also prepare questions for the audience should listeners be unresponsive during the question-and-answer period.
8. Encourage class discussion of the students' observations of the lecturers' communication skills.
9. Draw students' attention to various aspects of their own presentation style through individual feedback and that generated by the whole class.

Caveats and Options

1. If two students wish to attend the same lecture, they must work together in observing the lecture and in presenting to the class; each should take an active listening and speaking role in the activity.
2. Have students who wish to go to more specialized lectures adapt their topic to the needs of a nonspecialist audience (if such is the case). Make sure students understand that their audience consists of their classmates and their presentations must be adapted to the particular needs of the group.
3. To decrease task complexity, ask students to present in small groups of four to five participants.

Contributor

Susan Parks is involved in ESL program administration and teacher training in Montreal, Canada. She is the co-author of On Track I *(Oxford).*

Generating Speech From Postage Stamps

Levels
Any

Aims
Talk to classmates about
what is depicted on
stamps

Class Time
Variable

Preparation Time
None

Resources
Postage stamps

This activity asks students to speak extemporaneously from a limited data source. Students sometimes feel as if they have nothing to say. Providing them with a prop—such as a postage stamp—and then showing them they can use this simple prop to generate language gives them some self-confidence when speaking an L2. Postage stamps provide a somewhat restricted array of subjects: Famous people, flags, flowers, buildings, and so forth. However, if the information provided on the stamps is exploited well, considerable speech can be generated.

Procedure

1. Have students bring postage stamps to class (or you can supply them). Students may either work with their own stamps or with stamps they have exchanged with other students.
2. Using a stamp as "data," have students describe what is on the stamp to the whole class, including such information as the country or area of origin, the colors, the denomination, what the stamp is worth in U.S. money, what the stamp depicts in terms of pictures, diagrams, or people, and the significance of the items depicted. (Famous persons are especially good because the presenter should be able to discuss who the person is and why that person has been honored by being put on a postage stamp.)
3. Following each student's presentation, encourage the class to ask questions of the presenter. This procedure presents you with an opportunity to teach students how to ask appropriate kinds of questions. If the presenter cannot answer a specific question, call for volunteers. If there are no answers, direct the class or an individual

274

student to find the answer from appropriate sources either in the classroom, library, or some other source.

Caveats and Options

1. It is helpful to set up a file of stamps for future use. A wall map showing the countries of the world is a helpful resource to point out places and countries that may not be familiar to all of the students.
2. A whole period may be devoted to this type of exercise, or a teacher may elect to have two or three students speak at each class session.
3. Instead of one student making an oral presentation to the rest of the class, have students work in small groups.
4. Have students write descriptions of the "data" contained on the stamps, either individually or in groups in which the participants discuss what should go in the written versions.

Contributor

Ted Plaister taught in the Department of ESL, University of Hawaii, for 24 years. He has also taught in Thailand, Japan, Micronesia, and American Samoa.

Speaking Time

Levels
High beginning +

Aims
Emphasize fluency over accuracy
Increase confidence when speaking

Class Time
5–10 minutes

Preparation Time
15–30 minutes

Resources
Chalkboard and chalk
Lined paper and pens
Pictures or handout

ESL learners are often shy about speaking because of the inaccuracies in their English. Even if the teacher tries to accommodate the students' silent period, it can be difficult to work with or evaluate the less active students. In an effort to encourage the students to express their ideas and their concepts fluently, the teacher can give them a chance to speak in front of the class on the topic of their choice. This activity focuses on speaking so that the students do not have to worry about spelling and structure.

Procedure

1. At the beginning of the term, announce to the students that they all will have an opportunity to speak in front of the group.
2. Put up a large calendar so that students can pick the date they prefer.
3. After the break of every class session, have one student come forward and speak about the topic he or she chose.
4. During the speech, you should sit in the audience.
5. Have each student speak for about 5 minutes.
6. Have the other class members hold their questions and comments until the speaker has finished. (You and other students can help the speaker answer overly difficult questions.)

Caveats and Options

1. After each speech, give the speaker some feedback. (Psychologically, compliments should come before criticism so as to encourage the students.)

2. After every student takes a turn (if there is time left), students may have a second opportunity to speak. It is the element of choice here that helps put the learner at ease and gives them more control over the speaking event.

Contributor

Giang Vo teaches ESL to adults in Ottawa, Canada. She has been teaching in this field for 10 years.

♦ Spoken English for Academic Purposes

Poster Carousel

Levels
Intermediate +

Aims
Form and respond
spontaneously to
questions on
professional or
academic topics

Class Time
Two 90-minute classes

Preparation Time
1 hour

Resources
Research articles
Large paper for
flipcharts
Poster pens
Rulers
Scotch tape
Large classroom

Presentation via poster is increasingly common at professional and academic conferences as an alternative means of disseminating research findings. It makes specific demands regarding how the presenter and visitor interact. Poster Carousel has students extract information from a research article to create a poster that is both striking and easily read. By having students view and discuss a set of posters, the activity provides intensive practice for both presenter and visitor in coping with questions under time constraints.

Procedure

1. Find suitable short research articles (one for each pair of students).
2. Divide the class into pairs and give each pair an article to read.
3. Have partners agree on a summary of content and findings in the form of a poster, using no more than two flipchart sheets of paper.
4. Tape or pin the finished posters on the classroom wall far enough apart to allow viewing and discussion without interfering with a neighboring pair of students.
5. Have one student from each pair stand by their poster to respond concisely to any questions or points raised by other students visiting the poster. (However, hosts should not initiate discussion or explanation.)
6. Have the other member of each pair join the pool of visitors who each go to a different station every 5 minutes or so to read and absorb the information in the poster. Encourage the visitors to raise questions and points of disagreement with the presenter.

7. Signal (with a bell or whistle) when time is up and have each visitor move on clockwise to the next poster in the carousel.
8. Repeat the timed cycle as many times as necessary for each visitor to view and ask questions about all the posters.
9. Have the members of the original pairs then switch roles, so that the ones who have been answering questions can work their way around the carousel as visitors.
10. Monitor the question-and-answer interaction and make notes of points to comment on in plenary at the end of the activity.

Caveats and Options

1. As time allows, allocate more time to preparation work on poster design skills or to extended debriefing on questioning skills (based on your monitoring notes).
2. The rotation around the carousel gives the presenter experience in natural rehearsal by asking him to explain points asked many times by many visitors. This can reduce dependence on a minilecture. At the same time, visitors become more fluent in formulating and following up with questions based on newly read information.

Contributors

Tony Lynch heads the English for academic purposes (EAP) section at the Institute for Applied Language Studies (IALS), Edinburgh, United Kingdom, and has written books on EAP listening and speaking. Joan Maclean is responsible for the English for medicine section at IALS and is the author of books and articles on international medical communication.

Class Talk

Levels
High beginning +

Aims
Talk as much as
possible in class
Develop cooperation
skills in small groups
Increase and practice
vocabulary

Class Time
30–40 minutes

Preparation Time
10–60 minutes

Resources
None

A lot of in-class language activity is generated by the teacher, especially at low levels. Class Talk gives the students the opportunity to develop their own views on a topic and to interact with each other in a real-life situation: chatting about something. The activity allows shy students time to practice speaking skills and encourages cooperation among students of varying competence.

Procedure

1. At the beginning of the semester, have students organize themselves into small groups that will form anew each time this activity is conducted.

2. Generate topics for discussion in one of three ways:

   - Have the students suggest topics.
   - Prepare and suggest topics to the class.
   - Have students (or yourself) research and suggest topics related to their field of study (particularly in ESP situations).

3. Make sure each group has a different topic, which can vary depending on the level of the class and the interests of the students. Some classes have produced topics such as:

   - Men and women are equal.
   - Pollution is a serious problem.
   - Living in a city is fun.
   - There are not enough facilities at college.
   - Term holidays are too long.
   - Education means more than studying.
   - Computer integrated manufacturing is necessary for future growth.
   - An engineer's job has many aspects to it.

- Working for a small company is better than working for a big company.

4. Discuss strategies for presenting topics in English and encourage group members to agree or disagree with the ideas of other members during the upcoming discussion. Let students know that after each group discussion, one member will be chosen to present the groups' ideas to the class. (It is important not to tell the group in advance who is going to speak in front of the class so that all students take part in the group discussion.)

5. Have one member of each group present the ideas to the others for a group discussion lasting about 12–15 minutes, while you listen and circulate among groups to help with language problems. (Try to intervene as little as possible so students are encouraged to speak freely.)

6. Once the time has expired, choose one person from each group to stand up and present the group's ideas to the whole class for 2–3 minutes.

7. Encourage students in the class to ask questions of the presenter or the group to further probe the positions and interest of group members.

Caveats and Options

1. Class Talk can be used as a diagnostic tool to discover the strengths and weakness of students (e.g., agreeing, disagreeing, explaining, persuading).

2. In ESP situations, this can be a helpful revision activity where students discuss topics they have already studied in their subject area.

Contributor

Lindsay James Miller is a lecturer in the English Department at City Polytechnic of Hong Kong. He has taught English in Europe, the Middle East, and Southeast Asia for the past 13 years.

Considering the Job Market

Levels
Intermediate +

Aims
Think about careers
Practice comparative
forms communicatively

Class Time
1 hour

Preparation Time
1 hour

Resources
List of common
professions (see
Appendix below)

Many students are interested in studying ESL for instrumental purposes. This activity provides authentic information about professions that may be useful to students who are interested in becoming better prepared to make appropriate career decisions. It promotes conversational fluency and critical thinking while helping students make connections to the world outside the classroom.

Procedure

1. Find information about common professions including the following information:

   - annual earnings
   - job security
   - relative degree of prestige
   - employee satisfaction
   - employment outlook for immediate future
   - ratio of men to women . . . .

   Information of this kind is published in a concise table each year by a number of popular magazines (e.g., *Money Magazine*, *Money Digest*, *Parade Magazine*).

2. Prepare a series of handouts for students. The first handout should list 50 or more of the most common professions in random order.

3. Ask students to work collaboratively in groups of two or three to rank the professions according to one (or more) of the following criteria:

   - prestige
   - degree of verbal interaction with the public
   - likelihood of being filled by women

- salary
- physical demands
- level of education
- degree of competency in writing (or reading, or speaking, or listening)
- attractiveness
- computer skill required
- amount of travel or international sojourn required

4. Encourage the students to explain to each other and to keep track of the reasons behind the decisions they reach while they are engaged in this series of ranking activities.
5. If your aim is to generate personal impressions and opinions, provide a slightly reworded handout that asks students to evaluate professions according to the following criteria:

   - professions that they think should pay a higher salary than they currently do
   - those that currently are more likely to be filled by men but that they think a women could perform just as well
   - those that they think should carry higher prestige than they currently do

6. After students have had a chance to compare and discuss a number of these professions in pairs, provide them with opportunities to compare their work with other members of the class.

Caveats and Options

1. You may want to give students original information from an authentic source (e.g., from one of the magazines listed above).
2. You can then have students compare their own responses, rankings, personal preferences, and impressions with descriptive information available from the authentic sources.
3. An authentic source that is useful for generating the first handout about jobs in the United States and Canada appears in the February 1992 issue of *Money Magazine* (Branch & Luciano, pp. 68–69). These authors include a table that lists the top 100 professions in

their discussion along with the descriptive information referred to above.

4. Another option is to follow a different format in constructing the handouts. Students might be asked to fill in a survey for each of the 50 professions using the familiar Likert scale questionnaire format (see Appendix below).

5. Set aside class time for students to work in pairs as they try to list and discuss some of the responsibilities that are faced by people who work in these various professions.

6. You can also ask students to consider some of the following:

- What does a person who works in this profession do?
- To whom are they responsible?
- What is expected of them?
- What are some reasons one might have for wanting to enter into this profession?
- What are some of the problems encountered by people who work in this profession?
- What are their realistic career prospects?
- How much money are people in this profession likely to make?

7. You can extend class discussion to cover topics such as elaborations of the job responsibilities of certain professions, issues involved in becoming a member of particular professions, predictable hurdles, and so forth.

8. You can invite a guest speaker who works in a profession of interest to the class. Some students might be interested in developing an in-class oral report on one of the professions.

9. Have students conduct surveys with native speakers similar to the ones described above outside of class and report on the results in class.

References and Further Reading

Branch, S., & Luciano, L. (1992, February). America's best jobs. *Money Magazine*, pp. 68–69.

Klippel, F. (1987). *Keep talking: Communicative fluency activities for language teaching*. New York: Cambridge University Press.

Appendix: Sample Survey

Directions: Select one of the professions from the master list and circle one response each for Items A–G. Once you have completed responses for your first selected profession, consider another profession. Continue in this way until you have considered all of the professions on the list. Your key to the responses is:

Strongly agree	Agree	Neutral	Disagree	Strongly disagree
(SA)	(A)	(N)	(D)	(SD)

A. This profession pays an excellent salary.
    (SA) (A) (N) (D) (SD)

B. This profession calls for many years of formal education.
    (SA) (A) (N) (D) (SD)

C. There are a lot of women working in this profession.
    (SA) (A) (N) (D) (SD)

D. This profession carries a high degree of prestige.
    (SA) (A) (N) (D) (SD)

E. This profession is physically demanding.
    (SA) (A) (N) (D) (SD)

F. This profession calls for a lot of interaction with the public.
    (SA) (A) (N) (D) (SD)

G. This profession calls for a high degree of competency in writing (or reading, or speaking, or listening).
    (SA) (A) (N) (D) (SD)

Contributor

John M. Murphy is Associate Professor of Applied Linguistics and ESL at Georgia State University. His publications have appeared in TESOL Journal, TESOL Quarterly, English for Specific Purposes, TESL Canada Journal, *and other L2 journals.*

English for Academic Purposes: Improving Oral Skills

Levels
High intermediate +

Aims
Improve oral skills
through presentations
and small groups/
cooperative learning

Class Time
20 minutes/student
presentation

Preparation Time
30–40 minutes

Resources
Chalkboard and chalk
or overhead projector
(OHP)

Students' ability to speak English often improves when they talk about their own fields of study, but in large classes, many students may not have enough opportunities to speak because of class size and cultural or personal differences. This activity allows students to choose their specific topics (based on reading and writing materials presented during class), present them as seminars, and answer questions. The small-group aspect of this activity allows reticent students the chance to speak more, with fewer people around them.

Procedure

1. Inform students at the beginning of the semester that they are responsible for a 20-minute oral presentation to the class on a topic in their field or a topic they are familiar with. The format includes:

   - 15 minutes for presenting their topic
   - 5 minutes for a question-and-answer period with other students and the instructor
   - acting and dressing appropriately

2. Model a presentation for the class, demonstrating the use of handouts, OHP, or other audiovisual aids.
3. Arrange a schedule of presentations for the semester so each student can research and plan a presentation well in advance. Also have students anticipate their audiovisual equipment and set-up needs.
4. During class sessions throughout the semester, have students read materials about their topic; discuss their readings and writing on their topics within small-group/cooperative learning sessions; and work on a portfolio of writing which reflects their readings and small group

discussions about their topic and other contemporary topics which interest them (e.g., national, international, campus).

5. Join each group periodically as an observer and facilitator, but speak as little as possible unless the group bogs down. Encourage students to help each other with suggestions about the reading and writing assignments, and to have informal debates and arguments during discussions of the topics.

6. Conduct presentations on a regular basis throughout the semester according to schedule.

7. Evaluate the presentations using an evaluation form for each student to assess professional behavior; use of English (including pronunciation, intonation, fluency, style, and volume); organization of presentation; use of aids; and handling of questions. Give an overall grade with comments.

Caveats and Options

Averaging multiple assessments of the presentations (e.g., by graduate assistants) and discussing the strengths and weaknesses of presentation skills with students are useful evaluation procedures.

Contributor

Arlene Schrade received her PhD in Foreign Language Education from Ohio State University and is currently Professor of Education at the University of Mississippi in the United States.

◆ Interviews and Questioning Cross-Cultural Contact Assignments

Levels
Any

Aims
Use functional
classroom language
outside class
Develop insider view of
English-speaking culture
Collect facts/opinions
on a topic with
individual oral
interviews
Learn new words and
idioms

Class Time
1½ hours

Preparation Time
30 + minutes/contact
assignment

Resources
English-speaking
contacts

A contact assignment gives students license to ask questions that they may not otherwise have the courage to ask a native English speaker. If conducted with someone from another culture, the contact assignment gives students insight into their own culture as well as others. It thus provides grounds for a comparison of cross-cultural behavior and values. Because some topics are universal (e.g., the broad topic of family and relationships, as opposed to, say, the narrow topic of U.S. football), the contact assignment can promote an understanding of the commonality of human needs and the diverse practices by which these needs are met.

Procedure

1. Choose a suitable topic and develop a set of questions for students (interviewers) to ask contact persons (interviewees).
2. Demonstrate and have students practice interview techniques in class.
3. Instruct students to conduct an interview with one or more contact persons. Whenever possible, have students audiotape the interview. In an English-speaking environment, encourage ESL students to find contacts who have lived most of their lives in the target culture.
4. Give students adequate time to complete their interviews.
5. Instruct students to take notes after the interview (from the audiotape or from memory), and from those notes, discuss their findings in small groups in class.
6. Collect the recorded interviews and evaluate them for fluency, accuracy, and appropriateness.
7. Have each student follow the informal report with a prepared speech to the whole class (e.g., a 3-minute summary of the interview).

Caveats and Options

1. You may omit steps depending on the students' level and the language functions in focus.
2. You may wish to provide sample opening gambits for students to use when approaching potential contact persons. Point out that employing certain verbal and nonverbal listening behaviors may make the interviewee feel more comfortable (e.g., nodding, maintaining eye contact, repeating key phrases, asking follow-up questions).
3. Warn students to test out the tape recorder before the interview and to record the entire interview without stopping the recorder.
4. Provide students with sample closing gambits to end the interview.
5. Sample topics may include eating habits, a typical day in the life of the interviewee, educational background, shopping habits, or other topics interesting to your particular group.
6. The following are options for advanced students:

   - Brainstorm topics and questions and discuss the appropriateness of questions relative to contact persons differing in age, marital status, sex, level of education, occupation . . . .
   - Write a verbatim transcription of the interview.

Contributor

Marsha Chan teaches ESL at Mission College in Santa Clara, California in the United States. She has published a book and videotapes on pronunciation and authored articles on oral communication.

Rank Order

Levels
Any

Aims
Make choices
State, explain, and
defend choices publicly
Listen attentively and
nonjudgmentally
Ask follow-up questions
for clarification and
elaboration

Class Time
1 hour initially; 15-
minute periods
thereafter

Preparation Time
30–60 minutes

Resources
Paper and note cards

Making choices among competing alternatives is a daily activity. Some choices are minor decisions: "Shall I wear my blue or my white sweater or should I wear the green plaid jacket instead?" Others are major decisions: "Should I buy a car or save my money for a college education?" The first step of this exercise demonstrates that many issues require thoughtful consideration. The second interactive step allows students to verbalize their priorities in English and offer their partners a chance to ask follow-up questions.

Procedure

1. Write a list of 15–40 multiple choice questions suitable to your students' ages, experience, range of vocabulary, and linguistic development.
2. Provide three or four alternative answers to each question and make some questions easier to answer than others.
3. Some sample questions might be:

   - What color do you like best?
     red
     blue
     black
   - Which of these ages do you think (or imagine) is the best?
     birth to 18
     18–40
     40–65
   - Which of the following people would you rather dance with?
     your mother (father)
     your teacher
     a stranger

- Which is least important to you in choosing a spouse?
  income
  age
  appearance
- If you were abandoned on a deserted island, which book would you find the most useful?
  a dictionary of the English language
  a history of world civilization
  the Bible or other religious book

2. Pass out the list of questions for a homework assignment. Have students rank the answers to each question from best to worst. (Explain that students must be prepared to explain their preferences and ranking for each question.)
3. Duplicate several sets of the questions from the list on separate cards or slips of paper.
4. At the next class meeting, select an able student (or call for a volunteer) with whom to demonstrate the following interactive task:

- Sit face-to-face with the student.
- With a stack of question cards face down in front of you, read the first card and the possible answers to the student.
- Model the verbal and nonverbal behaviors that you wish the students to emulate as they respond (e.g., smile and give eye contact to your partner, and ask follow-up questions such as "Why do you like blue better than black?" or "Which color do you like second best?" or "How is blue more comforting than red?").
- Avoid pulling the focus away from the speaker by saying things like, "Well, I don't like blue. I like black better than red."

5. Explain the procedures above to the class and point out the specific behaviors (verbal and/or nonverbal) and linguistic structures that you wish the students to practice.
6. Pair off students and give each pair a set number of cards.

7. Have students take turns drawing the top card, asking their partner the printed questions and following up with other appropriate questions.

8. When all the questions have been answered, have the pairs exchange question cards with each other.

9. Circulate among the groups to assist students in expressing their ideas on a question and assist their partners in asking appropriate follow-up questions.

Caveats and Options

1. Preteach question, clarification, and elaboration strategies at the level of your students' ability (e.g., expressing comparatives and superlatives, choices and preferences, reasons and results).

2. For beginning-level classes, you may want to limit the questions to certain grammatical or lexical forms. You may also want to emphasize pronunciation and grammatical form while monitoring beginners.

3. For more advanced students, the questions could comprise a variety of linguistic forms, including hypothetical situations requiring conditional sentences and critical thinking. Monitor the advanced students' use of variety in follow-up questions. You may also model and expect advanced students to practice additional communication strategies such as giving relevant comments, paraphrasing, and summarizing.

4. Instead of grouping students in pairs, try grouping them in triads. One student is the interviewer/listener, one is the speaker/respondent, and the third is the observer. An uninvolved observer may watch the behaviors of the other two better than observing him/herself.

References and Further Reading

Simon, S. B., Howe, L. W., & Kirschenbaum, H. (1972). *Values clarification: A handbook of practical strategies for teachers and students*. New York: Hart.

Contributor

Marsha Chan teaches ESL at Mission College in Santa Clara, California in the United States. She has published a book and videotapes on pronunciation and authored articles on oral communication.

Rotating Group Interviews

Levels
Any

Aims
Use English in a
nonthreatening,
communicative way
Build confidence and
fluency through
questioning techniques

Class Time
15 minutes

Preparation Time
None

Resources
None

Teachers of large classes rarely get a chance to hear individual students use what they are learning, and students in large classes rarely get a chance to direct questions to their peers or teacher. This activity addresses both these concerns. Students' affective filters (Krashen, 1982) are lowered because the students are not standing in front of the class alone (they stand in groups of four), and they have already prepared their questions at home. Student investment in and motivation for the task are enhanced because the teacher is not merely asking display questions but is handing the questioning power over to students.

Procedure

1. Divide students into groups of four.
2. For each class period, have a different group prepare questions at home, using the lexical items, grammar points, or functions taught that week in class. Questions can be as simple as "How often do you ... ?" for practicing adverbs of frequency, or more advanced, such as, "What do you think of Mr. Clinton?" (or another famous person), to practice such functions as expressing opinions.
3. Have each student in the group prepare five questions: three to ask fellow students and two to ask the teacher. (Students usually love hearing about the teacher and in this activity the teacher loses the "teacher face" and becomes a "normal person." In the process, students get input from a native English speaker.)
4. Have the chosen group come to the front of the class.
5. Have one member of the group pose a question to any student in the class (that student should stand also).

6. After answering the question, have the student from the audience return the question with "How about you?" (or something more imaginative) and sit down.
7. Continue the above steps until all students in the group have gotten to ask their questions, including the two to the teacher.
8. Sit in one of the standing student's desks and don't interrupt unless a question is unintelligible or confusing.
9. Choose four different students for the next class and continue the process over several periods until all students in the class to have had a chance to come up to the front and ask questions.

References and Further Reading

Krashen, S. (1982). *Principles and practices in second language acquisition*. Oxford: Pergamon.

Contributor

Lesley Koustaff has been working in Japan for 9 years. She is Associate Professor at Chikushi Jogakuen University, Fukuoka, Japan.

Community Agency Visits

Levels
Low intermediate +

Aims
Communicate in English
in the target community

Class Time
2–3 hours

Preparation Time
3 hours

Resources
Information brochures
from local government
agencies

College-bound students in intensive English programs are often isolated from the U.S. culture at large. It is easy for teachers to say "get out there and mingle" but hard for students to know how and where to begin. To increase knowledge of Americans and U.S. society, students are introduced to various agencies which form the basis of local communities (e.g., police department, fire department, parks and recreation, social services, unemployment, health clinics) through brochures provided by local government. This activity allows students to learn directly about services and activities available to local residents and learn indirectly about the framework of U.S. society. Using their oral skills to plan their visits and gather and share information with others can be very beneficial. The teacher's role ceases after the preparation phase as students embark in small groups into the community. This increases student responsibility and involvement while promoting solidarity among classmates.

Procedure

1. Have students select two or three agencies they would like to learn more about and rank them in order of preference.
2. Based on the preferences, assign small groups of students to go to the agencies. (Interest and motivation are tied closely in this assignment, so take care in making group assignments.)
3. Phone the agencies to explain the activity and set up appointments for student visits. (Be sure to locate a contact person who will speak with students and who is available for students to contact when confirming the appointment.)
4. Write up individualized instructions for each student, giving the agency's name, address, phone number, contact person, appoint-

ment time, and other group members. The instructions should also outline pre- and postvisitation procedures (see Appendix below).

5. As a problem-solving activity, have groups work out the details of their excursion (e.g., location, transportation).

6. Have students make a list of questions to guide their interview with the contact person. The groups should also identify and discuss any expectations they may hold about the agency they will visit.

7. Have one student from each group call the contact person and confirm the appointment. (Allow students to place this call during class time to add excitement and underscore the reality of the project.)

8. Be sure and address the pragmatic aspects of language necessary for this assignment (e.g., how to use the phone and confirm the appointment politely; how to conduct an informal interview; how to end a conversation and offer thanks gracefully). Do not assume that students will employ the interactive style that Americans understand as attentiveness. You should discuss and model eye contact, gestures, and comments before the interviews take place.

9. Have students complete their visits and return to the classroom with their information and notes on the interaction.

10. Give students class time to discuss the information and impressions of the communicative experience in preparation for presentation to the whole class.

Caveats and Options

1. For a more integrated approach, have students write the agencies to confirm appointments, and request written information (which can become reading material and a springboard for more informed questioning in the interviews).

2. Have students discuss their trip through taped journals or written essays that incorporate their experiences with researched information about the agency.

3. Have the groups work toward a class goal of creating a handbook of services and activities relevant to international students in the community.

Appendix: Sample Community Agency Project

Agency: City Engineering, Municipal Building, 220 E. Third St.
Contact: John Freeman; Phone: 331-6417
Students: Abdulla Hassan & Dong Min
Date of Visit: 4/24, 9–10 a.m.

I. Preparation

   A. Decide how to get to the agency and back to class by 11 a.m.
   B. Make a map to the location.
   C. What questions will you ask? (enough to last the hour)
     1. _____
     2. _____
     3. _____
   D. What do you expect the agency to be like?
     1. _____
     2. _____
     3. _____
   E. Who will call to confirm the appointment?
   F. Call your contact person.

II. The Visit

   A. Be on time and have questions ready.
   B. Have a notepad and pencil and listen attentively.
   C. Expect to leave by 10 a.m.

III. After the Visit

   A. Make an outline about your visit.
     1. Describe the agency and contact person.
     2. Write answers to your prepared questions.
     3. Compare your expectations with the actual experiences.

Contributor

Rebecca Mahan-Taylor is an intensive English instructor at the Center for English Language Training at Indiana University. Her interests include pragmatics, cross-cultural communication, and the community as a teaching resource.

Personalities From Around the World

Levels
Low intermediate +

Aims
Generate classroom
interaction
Practice rising and
rising-falling intonation

Class Time
30 minutes

Preparation Time
2–5 minutes

Resources
Chalkboard and chalk
Roll of mailing labels or
name tags
Colored pen

This activity is an expansion of Klippel's (1987) Most Names Procedure. In this version, however, the students, rather than the teacher, generate the initial list of celebrity names to be incorporated into the activity. Getting students to generate the list of names for themselves helps ensure that the personalities discussed in class will be familiar to them. The activity incorporates students' background knowledge within classroom discourse in practicing yes/no question forms.

Procedure

1. Write on the chalkboard a list of categories of people from around the world and from different periods of history. Some sample categories are scientists, explorers, military leaders, religious figures, actors, sports figures, politicians, entrepreneurs, musicians, criminals, heroes, characters from mythology, painters, poets, and novelists.
2. Once the sample categories have been introduced, encourage students to suggest a few additional categories of their own (e.g., TV personalities, characters from fiction, fashion designers, teachers, martyrs, dictators, pop or rock stars).
3. When the chalkboard list is equal to or greater than the number of students in the class, have each of the students select one of the categories.
4. When the categories have been divided up, distribute a set of 5–10 blank mailing labels (eventually to be used as name tags) to each of the students.
5. At this point, ask the individual students to generate a list of names representing well-known people from anywhere in the world (either

living or deceased, respected or infamous) who would fit their selected category.

6. Have the students write each of the individual names they generate onto one of the separate mailing labels. (Help with spellings and names as needed.)

7. After the students have each come up with 5–10 names, have them return the completed sets of labels to you. As the names are being handed in, quickly examine them and place a small ink dot on the ones that probably would be familiar to most of the members of the class.

8. Once the pool of names selected is equal to or slightly larger than the total number of students in the class, explain that you are going to begin sticking individual name tags (generated by some other member of the class) on each of the students' backs. (With some groups of learners, it may be a good idea to apologize ahead of time for the direct physical contact this stage of the procedure involves.)

9. Once you have placed name tags on each of their backs, ask the students to stand up and to begin circulating around the room.

10. Have each student try to find out whose name is on his or her back by asking yes/no questions. Their interlocutors are restricted to using either yes or no responses.

11. In order to get students to interact with as many different members of the class as possible, ask them to limit themselves to asking no more than three or four questions of each classmate.

12. Once a student is able to successfully identify the personality's name, offer to place a new one on his or her back from the pool of unused ones still available.

Caveats and Options

When the procedure has run its course, there are several ways of building upon these initial stages of the personalities activity. The following may provide additional language practice opportunities:

1. Students can discuss their questioning strategies for figuring out whose names were on their backs.

2. Students can generate lists of the vocabulary words, phrases, or sentences that came up spontaneously in their conversational interactions.
3. The whole class could practice accurate English-specific pronunciations of the personalities' names and professions (e.g., segmental sounds, stress, rhythm, and intonation).
4. Students can explain additional information concerning what they already know about some of these well known people.
5. In small groups, students can attempt to rank order the list of personalities according to the significance of their contributions to humanity.
6. Students can be encouraged to visit the library and find out more information concerning some of the personalities discussed in class.
7. Students might make in-class oral reports on the accomplishments or contributions of some of the personalities.
8. Students might develop a role play or simulation in which one of them plays the role of a TV talk show host who interviews a panel of famous or less known personalities from different periods of history.
9. Try to collect samples of spoken language students generate spontaneously during the fluency stages of the lesson, in order to use some of these samples in subsequent activities that focus on accuracy.

References and Further Reading

Firth, S. (1991) Pronunciation syllabus design: A question of focus. In P. Avery & S. Ehrlich (Eds.), *Teaching American English pronunciation* (pp. 173–183). New York: Oxford University Press.

Klippel, F. (1987). *Keep talking: Communicative fluency activities for language teaching*. New York: Cambridge University Press.

Morley, J. (1991). The pronunciation component in teaching English to speakers of other languages. *TESOL Quarterly, 25*, 481–520.

Murphy, J. M. (1991). Oral communication in TESOL: Integrating speaking, listening, and pronunciation. *TESOL Quarterly, 25*, 51–75.

Contributor

John M. Murphy is Associate Professor of Applied Linguistics and ESL at Georgia State University. His publications have appeared in TESOL Journal, TESOL Quarterly, English for Specific Purposes, TESL Canada Journal, *and other L2 journals.*

Personal Possessions

Levels
Any

Aims
Discuss selves and
valued possessions

Class Time
20 minutes

Preparation Time
5 minutes

Resources
Items students bring to
class

There are many ways to contextualize grammar while promoting conversation skills and self-esteem. This task entails the use of grammatical constructions and conversational conventions in making introductions in a noncompetitive, group-building activity. In this activity, students talk about themselves and learn about each other in a low-risk environment while practicing structures and their functions in context. It may also promote the development of a sense of community in the classroom.

Procedure

1. Seat the students in a circle and then pair them off across language backgrounds and levels of proficiency if possible. (If your students have homogeneous language backgrounds, then pair them across levels of proficiency.)
2. Give the students an example of the task. For example, "My wedding and engagement rings are important to me because my husband, an artist, designed them. They each have a peak and valley which when put together make a smooth circle. Marriage has its peaks and valleys. Together my husband and I try to smooth them out." (Use simpler examples with lower level classes.)
3. Have students choose one, two, or three, items from among their own possessions which they feel describe them as a person.
4. Have them share these items with their partner, explaining why they have chosen the item and how it describes them. (Students may use as much detail as they wish.)
5. Next, have the other partner describe him/herself using the same process outlined in Steps 3, 4, and 5 above, selecting an item of personal importance and temporarily lending the selected item to the partner.

6. After the students describe each item, have them lend it temporarily to their partner, for the partner to use in the introduction (see Step 7).

7. After all students have exchanged items, have them introduce each other to the class. This changes the first person self-report statements to third-person descriptions (e.g., "These are her wedding and engagement rings. They have . . . "). The descriptions are only limited by the students' imaginations and the items in their possession.

Caveats and Options

1. This activity is ideal for the first day of class for intermediate or advanced students or 3–4 weeks after the term starts for lower level students.

2. Time limits should be set in advance.

3. After sharing the information orally, students may write a description of their partners.

4. You can build in an active listening step in which the listening partner repeats back to the speaking partner the content of what was said, for example: "Those are your wedding rings and engagement rings . . . . " This step provides good preparation for the introduction of partners described in Step 7 above. It also sets up a context in which the learners use the second person singular.

5. Beginning-level students may use only one item if time limits are restricted. You may wish to introduce specific grammar patterns, such as "I chose _____ because _____."

6. It is essential to circulate among the students to keep them on task. In addition, for beginning-level students, the vocabulary and grammar may be challenging.

Contributor

Adelaide Heyde Parsons, Professor of TESOL/ESOL, has more than 20 years of experience in K–12, adult, and postsecondary education. Her main interest is affective language learning techniques and strategies.

Introducing a Classmate

Levels
Low intermediate +

Aims
Practice in eliciting
information for oral
presentations

Class Time
Variable

Preparation Time
30–60 minutes

Resources
Questionnaire and
Question Sheet (see
Appendices below)

This activity entails asking questions and recording answers in a brief, understandable way. It provides practice in interviewing skills, helps classmates get to know each other on a more personal basis, and facilitates the sharing of that information with other students. Students play the parts of interviewer and interviewee.

Procedure

1. Have students work in dyads to interview each other.
2. To facilitate the process and to provide guidelines, provide the forms to fill out and questions to ask on a handout (see Appendices A and B).
3. Have students maintain eye contact with each other when eliciting information (i.e., they should read over the question to be asked, and then look at their partner when saying it).
4. To facilitate the class presentations, have students use brief notes with the information about their partners.
5. Tell the students to use the major headings from the questionnaire to jog their memories,(e.g., Sports—baseball; Talents—plays chess well; Music—enjoys rock as well as classical).

Caveats and Options

1. The exercise can take up a fair amount of time in a large class, so it may need to be scheduled over several days.
2. The interviews should take approximately 10–15 minutes, and presentation time about 5–10 minutes per student. Interviews may be held during one class period and the introductions at another.
3. When working with large classes, it may be more efficient to do the introductions in groups rather than introducing each student to the entire class.

4. As a follow-up activity, you may want to assign a written report for homework in which students write up the "data" on their partners, for example:

The student I interviewed is named Alfredo Silva. He was born in Mexico, but now lives in the United States. He came here with his family when he was eight years old. He lives with his parents and his five younger brothers and sisters. Alfredo likes to play soccer . . . .

Appendix A: Questionnaire

Name _____

        Family   First/Given   Nickname

Birthplace _____

Birthdate _____

Native Language _____

Other Languages _____

Family Members _____

Sports _____

Hobbies _____

Talents _____

Music _____

Ambitions _____

Current Employment _____

Travel _____

Appendix B: Question Sheet

Name
     What is your family name?
     What is your first or given name?
     Do you have a nickname?

Birthplace
     Where were you born?

Birthdate
     What is your birthdate? (or)
     When were you born?

Native Language
> What is your native language?

Other Languages
> What other languages do you speak?

Family Members
> Tell me about your family members.

Sports
> What sports do you like to watch?
> What sports do you like to play?

Hobbies
> Do you have any hobbies?

Talents
> Can you play a musical instrument?
> Can you draw or paint?
> Do you like to build models?
> Do you sew or knit?
> Can you sing?

Music
> What kind of music do you like to listen to?

Ambitions
> What would you like to do when you finish school?

Current Employment
> Do you have a job now? If so, describe what you do on your job.

Travel
> What places have you traveled to?
> What places would you like to travel to?

Contributor

Ted Plaister taught in the Department of ESL, University of Hawaii, for 24 years. He has also taught in Thailand, Japan, Micronesia, and American Samoa.

Also available from TESOL

All Things to All People
Donold N. Flemming, Lucie C. Germer, and Christiane Kelley

A New Decade of Language Testing Research:
Selected Papers from the 1990 Language Testing Research
Colloquium
Dan Douglas and Carol Chapelle, Editors

Books for a Small Planet:
An Multicultural/Intercultural Bibliography
for Young English Language Learners
Dorothy S. Brown

Common Threads of Practice:
Teaching English to Children Around the World
Katharine Davies Samway and Denise McKeon, Editors

Dialogue Journal Writing with Nonnative English Speakers:
A Handbook for Teachers
Joy Kreeft Peyton and Leslee Reed

Dialogue Journal Writing with Nonnative English Speakers:
An Instructional Packet for Teachers and Workshop Leaders
Joy Kreeft Peyton and Jana Staton

Discourse and Performance
of International Teaching Assistants
Carolyn G. Madden and Cynthia L. Myers, Editors

Diversity as Resource:
Redefining Cultural Literacy
Denise E. Murray, Editor

New Ways in Teaching Reading
Richard R. Day, Editor

New Ways in Teacher Education
Donald Freeman, with Steve Cornwell, Editors

Students and Teachers Writing Together:
Perspectives on Journal Writing
Joy Kreeft Peyton, Editor

Video in Second Language Teaching:
Using, Selecting, and Producing Video for the Classroom
Susan Stempleski and Paul Arcario, Editors

For more information, contact
Teachers of English to Speakers of Other Languages, Inc.
1600 Cameron Street, Suite 300
Alexandria, Virginia 22314 USA
Tel 703-836-0774 • Fax 703-836-7864